DAVID ALEXANDER

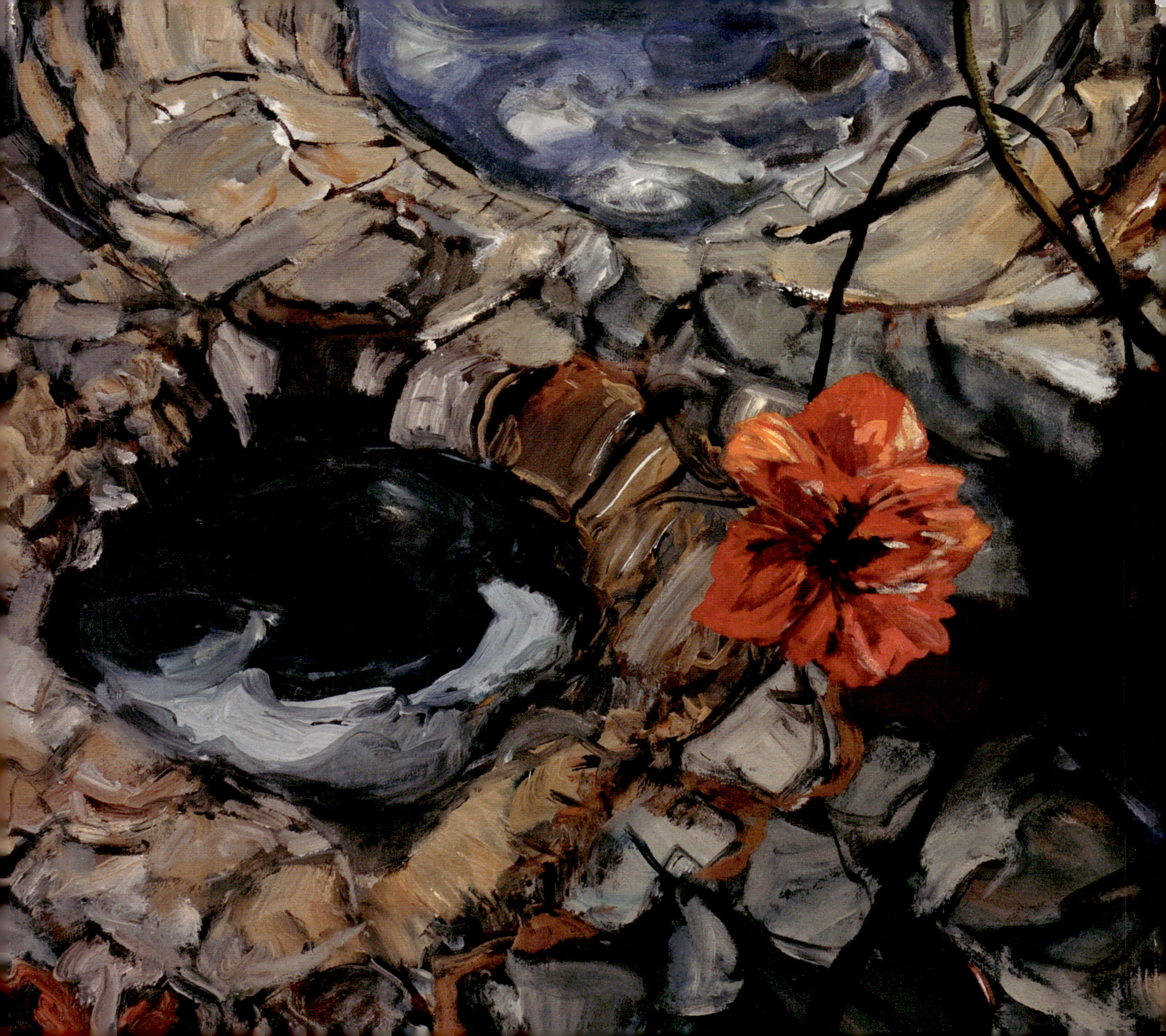

EDITED BY LIZ WYLIE

The Shape of Place

DAVID ALEXANDER

PUBLISHED FOR THE KELOWNA ART GALLERY BY McGILL-QUEEN'S UNIVERSITY PRESS
MONTREAL & KINGSTON · LONDON · ITHACA

ISBN 978-0-7735-4035-4

Legal deposit first quarter 2012
Bibliothèque nationale du Québec

Printed in Canada on acid-free paper.

McGill-Queen's University Press acknowledges the support of the Canada Council for the Arts for our publishing program. We also acknowledge the financial support of the Government of Canada through the Canada Book Fund for our publishing activities.

David Alexander : the shape of place / edited by Liz Wylie.

Published for the Kelowna Art Gallery by McGill-Queen's University Press.

Includes bibliographical references.
ISBN 978-0-7735-4035-4

1. Alexander, David, 1947– —Criticism and interpretation. 2. Landscape painting, Canadian. 3. Painting, Canadian—20th century. I. Wylie, Liz II. Kelowna Art Gallery

ND249.A44D38 2012   759.11   C2011-907817-1

This book was designed and typeset by studio oneonone in Adobe Garamond 10/14

Frontispiece: Detail from *Iceland's Earth's Kitchen*, 2001, acrylic on canvas, 58 × 52 in.

Page vi: Detail from *Rocky Scratch [Rockies]*, 2004, gouache and ink, 10.25 × 9.75 in.

Contents

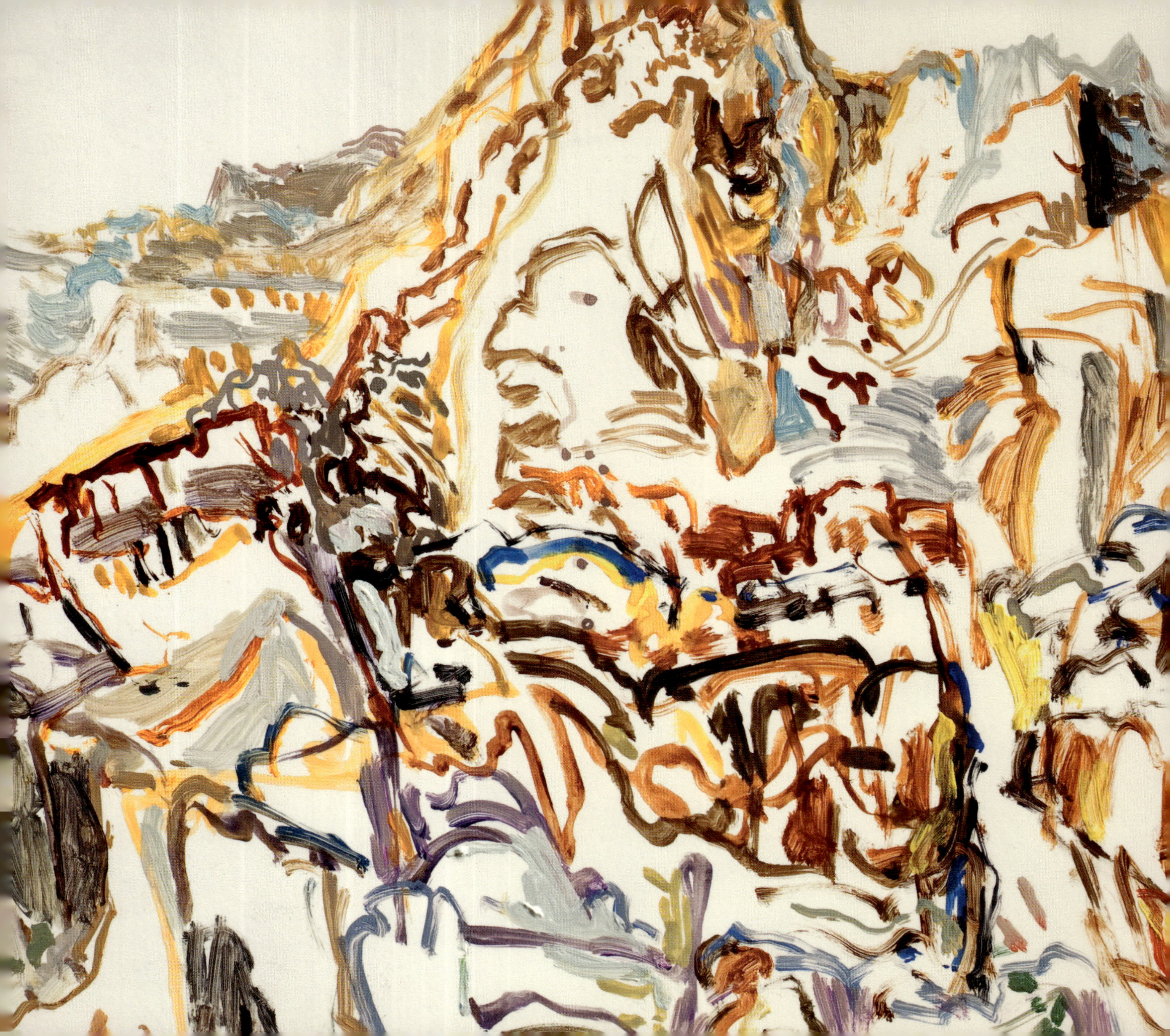

All works are by David Alexander, in the collection of the artist, and photographs credited to Yuri Akuney unless otherwise noted.

Acknowledgments

Creating this book on the work of David Alexander has been a team effort between the artist and Liz Wylie as both exhibition curator and book editor. It has taken us four years and the best part of it is that we're still speaking to each other. Our thanks go out to the people who have supported this project in a number of ways. First, to those who believed in the initial idea of this book. In early days, our behind-the-scenes enthusiasts were David Silcox and John O'Brian, to whom we are personally most grateful.

All of the people who came on board to participate in and support this project were motivated by their excitement about the artist's work, with no ulterior or base motives. This was truly inspiring to both of us. This includes our editor at McGill-Queen's University Press, Jonathan Crago, who has been such a pleasure to work with. The staff and members of the Board of the Kelowna Art Gallery were all also very supportive. It was a stretch for a small institution to take on such a major project, causing some staff members to work far beyond their normal workloads. Our heartfelt thanks go out to them as well as to artist Hannah Griffin, an undergraduate student at the University of British Columbia's Okanagan Campus in Kelowna when she completed a work placement course on this project in 2008 to 2009, during which she ably assisted the artist in preparing for this book.

We thank the staff at various public and private galleries who provided image files of works by other artists, used for comparative purposes throughout this volume.

We give a sincere thank you to the lenders of work to the traveling exhibition that this book accompanies. To the staff at the gallery venues for this show, we extend our appreciation and look forward feedback from the communities to which the show will travel. At the time this book is going to press, these include the Confederation Centre's Art Gallery (Charlottetown, PEI), the Tom Thomson Memorial Art Gallery (Owen Sound, Ontario), and the Esplanade Art Gallery (Medicine Hat, Alberta).

We offer our sincere thanks to David Alexander's dealers and their gallery staff: Tien Huang and Alissa Sexton at the Bau-Xi Gallery in Toronto and Riko Nakasone, Jennifer Johnson, and Tallie Thompson at Bau-Xi in Vancouver, Peter Robertson and Nomi Stricker at the Peter Robertson Gallery in Edmonton, Sherril Wallack and Dan Pellerin at the Wallack Galleries in Ottawa, and Fhen Huang, Judith Rinehart, and Kim Coulter at the Foster/White Gallery in Seattle, and to

Alexander's dealer Saskatoon, Darrell Bell. Thank you for your support.

We would also like to most gratefully acknowledge the vital contributions of the writers in this book. Each has brought his or her own experience and perspective to Alexander's work and we are pleased at the richness that this gathering of voices provides. We were thrilled and honoured when award-winning author Sharon Butala agreed to meet with Alexander and contribute an essay to this book. Her own writing on the prairie has been inspirational to both of us and her essay in this book about the artist's engagement with nature is moving and wonderful. We are grateful to be able to include a witty and engaging text about Alexander's work by the late Edmonton-based writer Gilbert Bouchard, written in 2008. Robert Enright has contributed one of his hallmark artist interviews. It allows readers the opportunity to hear the artist's voice as he is artfully drawn into conversation with someone who has spent years thinking about his work, as well as that of many other artists. Our colleague Ihor Holubizky reflects on Alexander's raw take on the landscape in relation to the work past artists produced when confronted with parts of the world that were new and exotic to them. Finally, writer and curator Aðalsteinn Ingólfsson recounts his own experience of being introduced to Alexander's work, and then having him visit Iceland in 1999 and 2002. This international perspective on Alexander's art lends a unique element to the book.

Both David Alexander and Liz Wylie have been saddened by the recent deaths of important senior Canadian artists in the last few years. These include Gordon Rayner, Richard Gorman, and David Bolduc. We salute their achievements.

David Alexander also remembers and honours the work of the late Paterson Ewen, and would also like to pay tribute to his friend the late American painter Stanley Boxer. He also acknowledges his colleague and friend at Emily Carr University, printmaker Rodney Konopaki, with whom he has had several creative collaborations, along with those of his artist colleagues in Saskatoon who still call him a friend.

Liz Wylie would like to mention the personal inspiration of her late colleague, art historian Robert Stacey, who loved art, landscape painting, and places, in particular, the magic of specific places rendered in visual form: something of what David Alexander's art is all about.

We are optimistic that this book will engender further appreciation of David Alexander's art, both in Canada and abroad. We hope that the words of the authors help stimulate shared discussion and individual contemplation of the paintings. Despite being considered moribund in many quarters, we still believe in the art book as a portal through which to look at art and experience its transformative effects.

DAVID ALEXANDER AND LIZ WYLIE

DAVID ALEXANDER

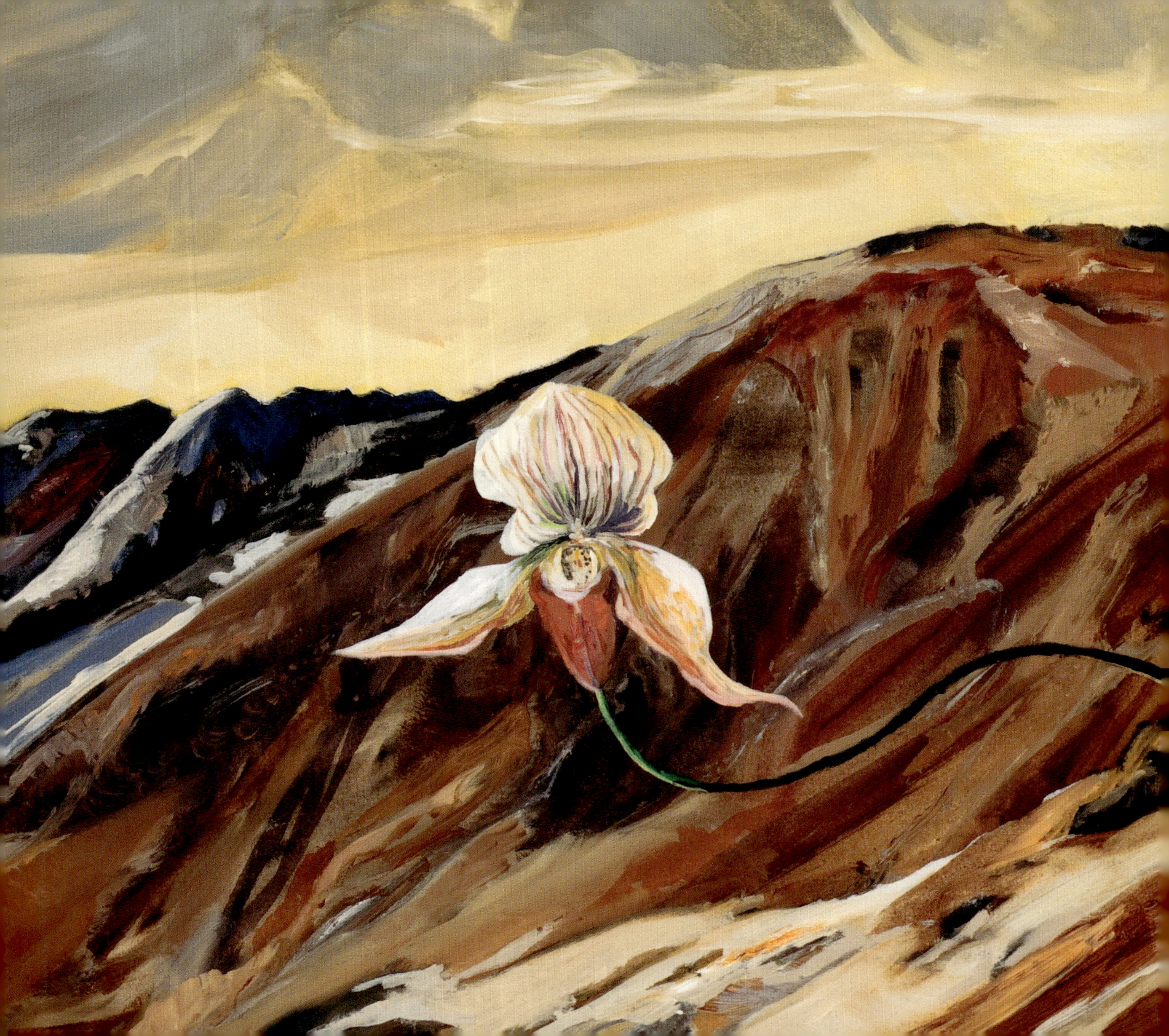

THE LANDSCAPE IS THE EVIDENCE

Liz Wylie

I believe in God, only I spell it Nature.
Frank Lloyd Wright

Did it first start and take hold in David Alexander when he was a boy, motoring up and down among the islands off the North West Coast in a tug boat with his father? With the land, sea, and sky constantly moving and changing around him, he was completely immersed in the natural world. He always loved to draw. At age fifteen he took over the bedroom his older brother had vacated; it became his first studio. He was also fed a steady diet of Emily Carr from a young age. Does all this add up to some kind of foolproof recipe to produce a Canadian landscape artist? It worked in his case: David Alexander went on to art school, earning a BFA and MFA, and established an international exhibiting career. He is now one of Canada's most well-known and admired living landscape painters: one of a handful of contemporary artists keeping the tradition of drawing outdoors on site alive, while extending the reach and role of that activity to make it a living, modern pursuit.

Really, the category "landscape" is too small and limited a term to describe nature as a subject for art, David Alexander's included. It reflects the pervasive human attitude to the natural world as something to be measured, owned, and exploited, rather than something to be viewed with respect and awe, and as inextricably connected with our selves. It is in this sense that the words fails us from the outset and will even obstruct and thwart our understanding and apprehension of the meaning of Alexander's art. A new word would need to be coined which could encompass and convey the notion of art as paying homage to one's experience of nature. It would describe not a simple visual representation of landforms, for example, but the kind of art that is a remembering and re-membering of a vital and humbling experience. It would speak the truth that we all recognize on some level: that nature is the only world we know and inhabit.

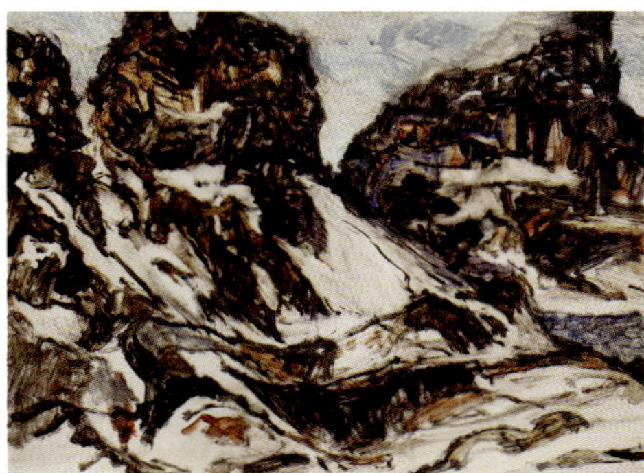

Rockies, Early Spring, 1999, gouache and ink, 9 × 12 in.

Opposite Detail from *Not Much Belongs in the Arctic,* 1998–9.

Alexander has long been attracted to remote places, especially those with very little human footprint. Going to new places to sketch, draw, and take notes, then returning to the studio to work on paintings is how he has kept himself energized and focused. He is a restless artist, one who cannot remain stimulated if staying in one place, needing constant movement in order to survive. Alexander's need to keep his work's edges sharp also feeds his desire to explore new terrains and locales. It is the thrill he takes in discovering new natural surroundings – icebergs in the Arctic, volcanoes in Iceland, the immensity of the Grand Canyon – that energizes his art and allows the viewer to share his raw delight and awe. As an artist, he is the polar opposite of Cézanne who, late in his life in Aix-en-Provence, wrote to his son that he could just sit in one spot and needed only to move his head a bit to the left or right to have an infinite variety of motifs for painting made available. This is not to say that nature cannot be captured close to home: as of the late fall of 2010, Alexander was at work on a new series of paintings inspired by the patterns, light, and shapes on the surface of a pond only a ten-minute drive from his home.

Alexander's work has undergone its own trajectory over the years. Recently, it seems less about the finished painting than the visibility of the artist *in* his painting: as viewers, we experience not only Alexander's portrayal of the landscape, but also his act of painting, foregrounded in intense, visceral ways. His work can look awkward, direct, raw, even lurid or unfinished. In contrast, his first professional paintings (beginning in the 1980s) were less challenging, and can seem rather decorative, even tame, in hindsight. In his early work, colours worked in pleasant harmonies with one another. He applied his paint loosely and thinly, and the paintings did not have a strong structure or reference to three-dimensionality. They were mostly about colour, surface, shape, and implied texture. It was in grappling with his various artistic influences that a route forward presented itself for Alexander. He needed to thoroughly digest and move beyond Emily Carr and come to terms with Monet. Slowly, his colours deepened and became richer, his paint got thicker, and his pictorial ideas took on more risk. It is worth noting that the landscape upon which he cut his teeth was the western Canadian prairie (Alexander lived in Saskatoon from 1980 to 2003). This is probably one

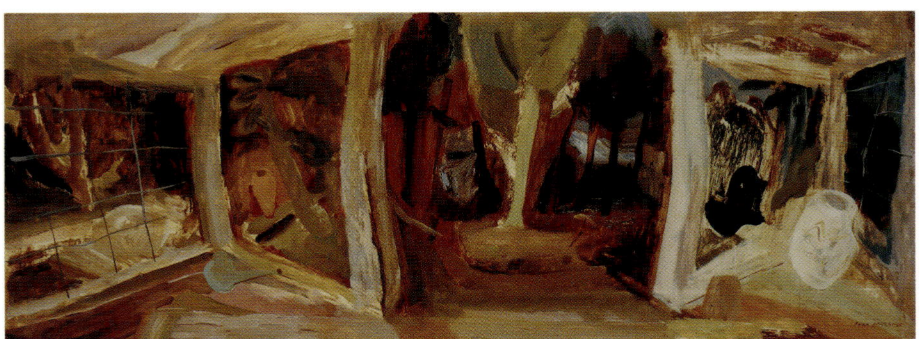

Ivon Hitchens, *Winter Stage*, 1936,
oil on canvas, 23.1 × 61.3 in.
© Tate, London 2011.

of the most challenging subjects for a landscape artist, with its low flat horizon line, often fairly featureless expanses, and massive cloud formations in the huge sky. But once he had found a way to paint the prairie, Alexander was ready for further explorations. He also kept up with urban travels to look at art, and in the 1980s and 1990s encountered and digested the work of American Philip Guston and the British artist Ivon Hitchens. It seems that part of Alexander's project or path involved first mastering all the rules and idioms of late modernist painting, before he could begin to bend and break them for his own purposes. Now he says he likes to work from a place of not-knowing: he needs to not know where he is or what he is doing to feel he is on the edge of something, to keep things exciting and challenging. "You keep learning how to deal with the problems. You keep needing conflict. Artists need to take on conflicts, it's where they live."[1]

Alexander works on a large scale and seeing the paintings is a uniquely pleasurable experience. His brand of hedonism is a northern one that channels artists like Ferdinand Hodler and Edvard Munch, not a warm Mediterranean mode of expression, as practiced by Matisse. But his hedonism is not unchecked or lazy; it has rigorous underpinnings. Perhaps the notion of an elevated spirit is more accurate, a notion that calls to mind the word *šamán* (the root for the word shaman from an indigenous Siberian language), meaning lifted or elevated. In shamanism's magical and religious metaphysical conception of the world and universe, the connection between humans and nature is absolute. The notion of elevation relates to the visions and ecstatic experiences that the shaman of each tribal unit undergoes. Many writers have likened the role of the contemporary artist to that of the shaman: effective at

healing, providing a portal between the different levels of the universe, a "way" for others. Although it may seem extreme and romanticized, there is something that rings true about this for David Alexander and his questing, his expression of what he has experienced "out there" in his paintings. We lack words – back to that dilemma again – for the experience of immersing oneself in nature: what *is* that encounter and what does it mean? From the outset we cannot pretend to know anything about the topic in the traditional sense. But the feeling that the viewer has from Alexander's work is unmistakable, even though it may be difficult to articulate.

Some of Alexander's most intense and riveting works are to be found in the sketchbooks he takes on his trips. The notions of freshness and spontaneity are clichés when it comes to sketches, but they still do apply to the immediacy and sheer breath of Alexander's *plein air* drawings. Particularly in his panoramic works that span a double-page spread, the sense of the artist being *in* the landscape is palpable.

Alexander tends to work in series, often based on a painting research trip somewhere, or a single motif that he wants to work out. Beginning in the 1980s, he made it a priority to travel as much as he could to places he wanted to paint: the near North of Ontario, the Canadian Arctic, Greenland and Iceland, northern Scotland, Japan, the Morris Graves Foundation in California, Argentina, and the Grand Canyon in Arizona. Each place that he has visited has required a different approach to render the ethos of the locale. He likes to arrive without preconceptions, and let his knowledge grow as he spends time in a place, usually walking, sometimes traveling by boat.

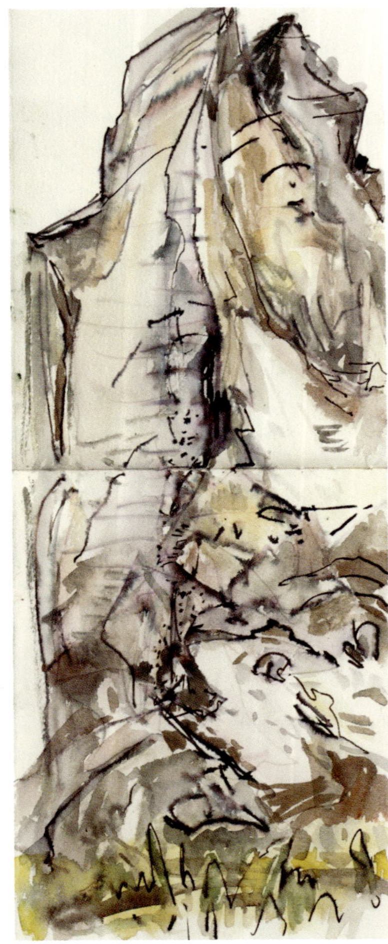

Above
Untitled [Valhalla, Slocan Valley], 2004,
ink and watercolour, 14.5 × 5.75 in.

Above right
East Coast [Newfoundland], 1996, gouache
and ink, 8.5 × 11 in.

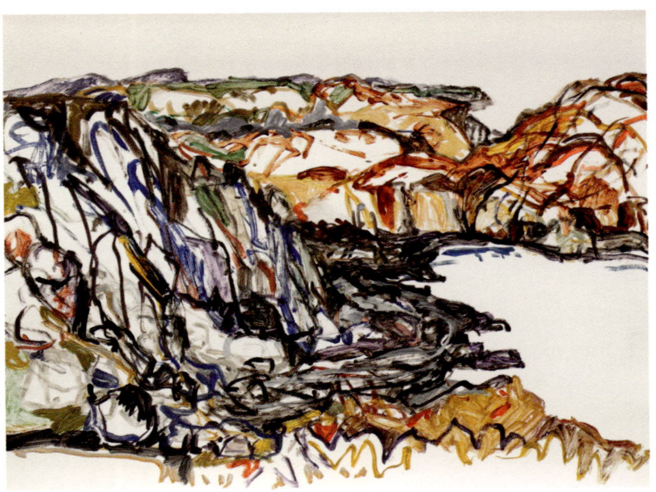

What is success for Alexander? It is not the feeling of satisfaction with any particular painting, as this eludes him. Is it
an exhibition career that now spans three decades? He says:
"Success and failure continuously go hand in hand as you
work on a painting. You fix and doctor the failures as you
go along until it is done."[2] The notion of ambition – career
ambition – does not seem to be something he spends a lot of
time thinking about. Even the notion of an audience for his
work, and their perceptions of it, seems amorphous to him.
He thinks and works alone. But what then is his place in
the spectrum of Canadian art, its history, and the incredible
diversity of the contemporary moment? Alexander is insis-
tently modern: he does not want to be viewed as a living
relic using methods from the past. He does not figure in a
recent tome given over to an examination of contemporary

approaches to the land in Canadian art,[3] one might assume, because he was not considered a postmodern artist. One could argue, however, that while he may not be rewriting the genre or method of landscape art, he is trying to breathe some life into it, to *personally* extend it.

With that said, one wonders what Alexander's artistic context would actually consist of, both in Canada and beyond its borders. In Canada, artists who work with the landscape in one way or another and do so with ambition and intelligence, are scattered from coast to coast to coast. A list of such varied artists would include Gregory Hardy, Eleanor Bond, Monica Tap, Carol Wainio, Medrie MacPhee, and Wanda Koop. Internationally, Kim Dorland, the Canadian artist now working in New York, has some parallels with Alexander in his work's forthright, almost aggressive depictions. Of course, one also thinks of Peter Doig, who also spent his childhood from age seven to twenty in Canada. Doig is arguably today's most well-known and widely exhibited artist working in landscape in a serious, engaged, and ambitious manner. He is more pictorial in his approach than is Alexander, however; things seem a little more literal in his paintings, and about a mood or a scene, less about a specific place and its history and geography. To work with landscape as a contemporary artist is a challenge in and of itself, and perhaps the most difficult aspect of that challenge is to have an audience who experiences your work in the present moment, for itself, and separate from the landscape tradition of the past.

The title of this essay was spoken by David Alexander one day in conversation about the traces of geological history, human migrations, and settlements, all of which leave their marks on the land. "The landscape is the evidence," he said, and I thought of the land as a scarred and marked body: not a new or original idea, but a powerful one nevertheless. In the end, it comes down to David Alexander walking around somewhere, sketching, then making paintings in his studio. And each painting can be seen as just a link between the one before it and the one that will follow it. In and of themselves, they are not yet what the artist hopes to achieve. Alexander comments: "You're never finished." One never finishes, time just runs out.

NOTES

1 David Alexander, in conversation with the author, 27 August 2010.

2 Ibid.

3 John O'Brian and Peter White, *Beyond Wilderness* (Montreal: McGill-Queen's University Press, 2007).

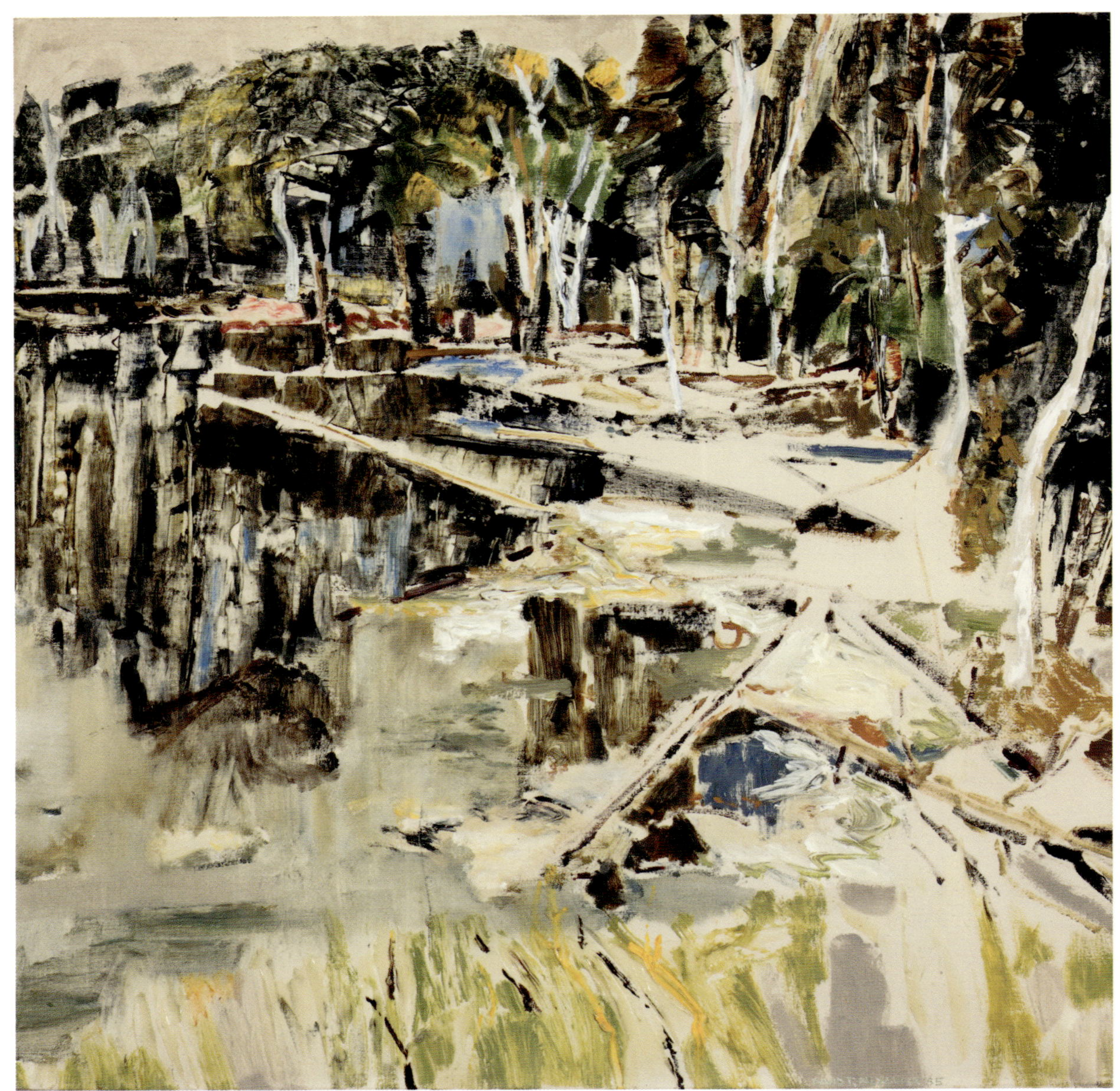

A Reflected Northern Saskatchewan Lake, 1985, acrylic on canvas, 47 × 47.5 in.

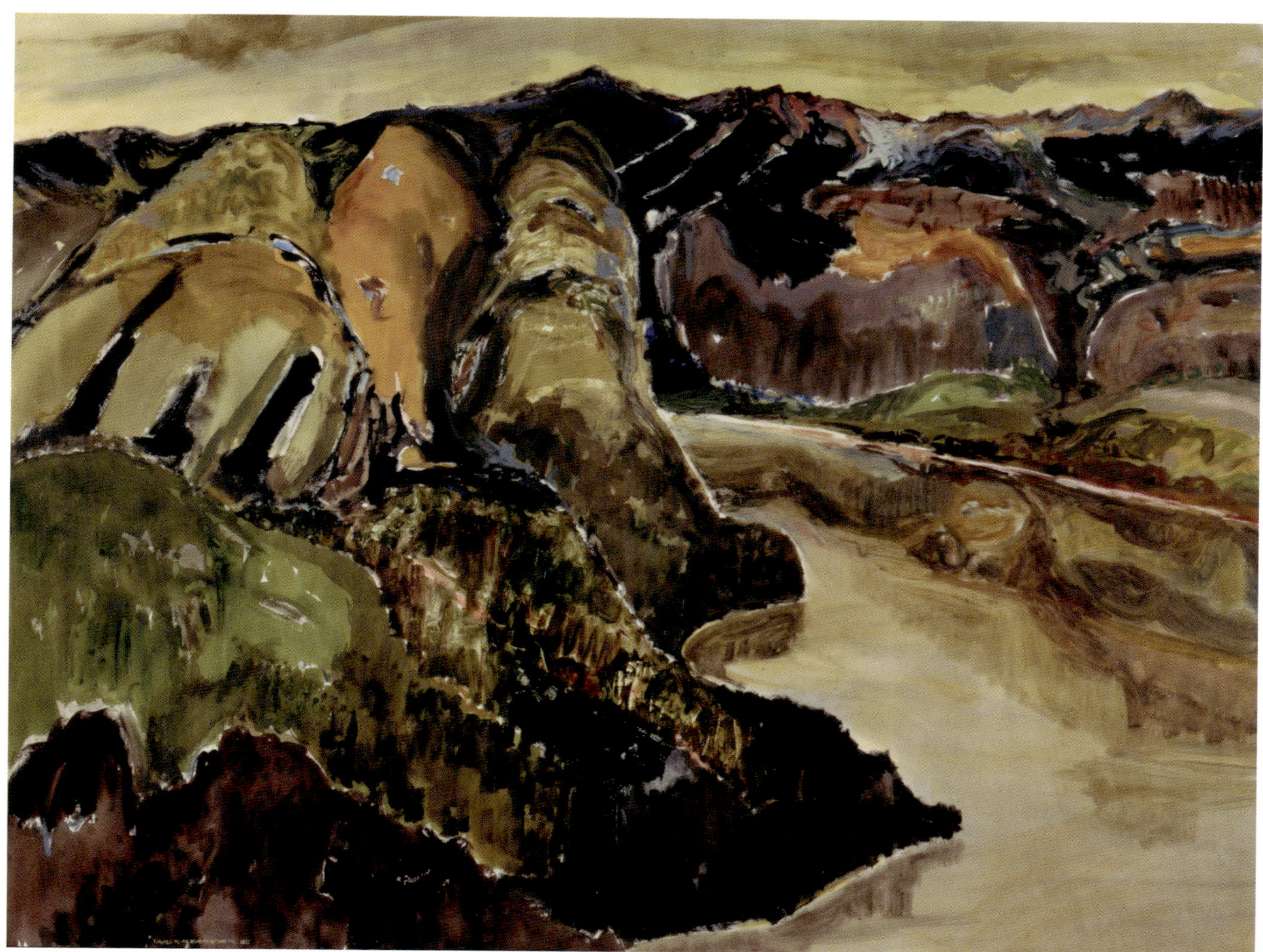

PLATE 2

Kokanee Grip, 1985, acrylic on canvas, 66 × 83 in.

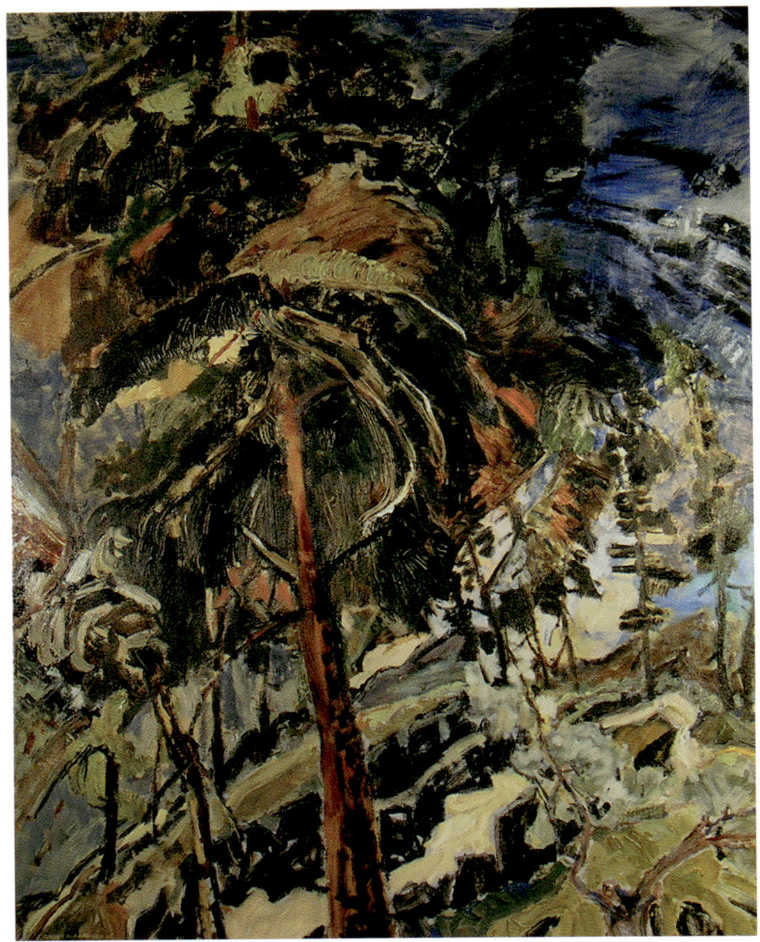

PLATE 3

Vorticose Trees (Old Guard), 1987, acrylic on canvas, 67.5 × 58 in.

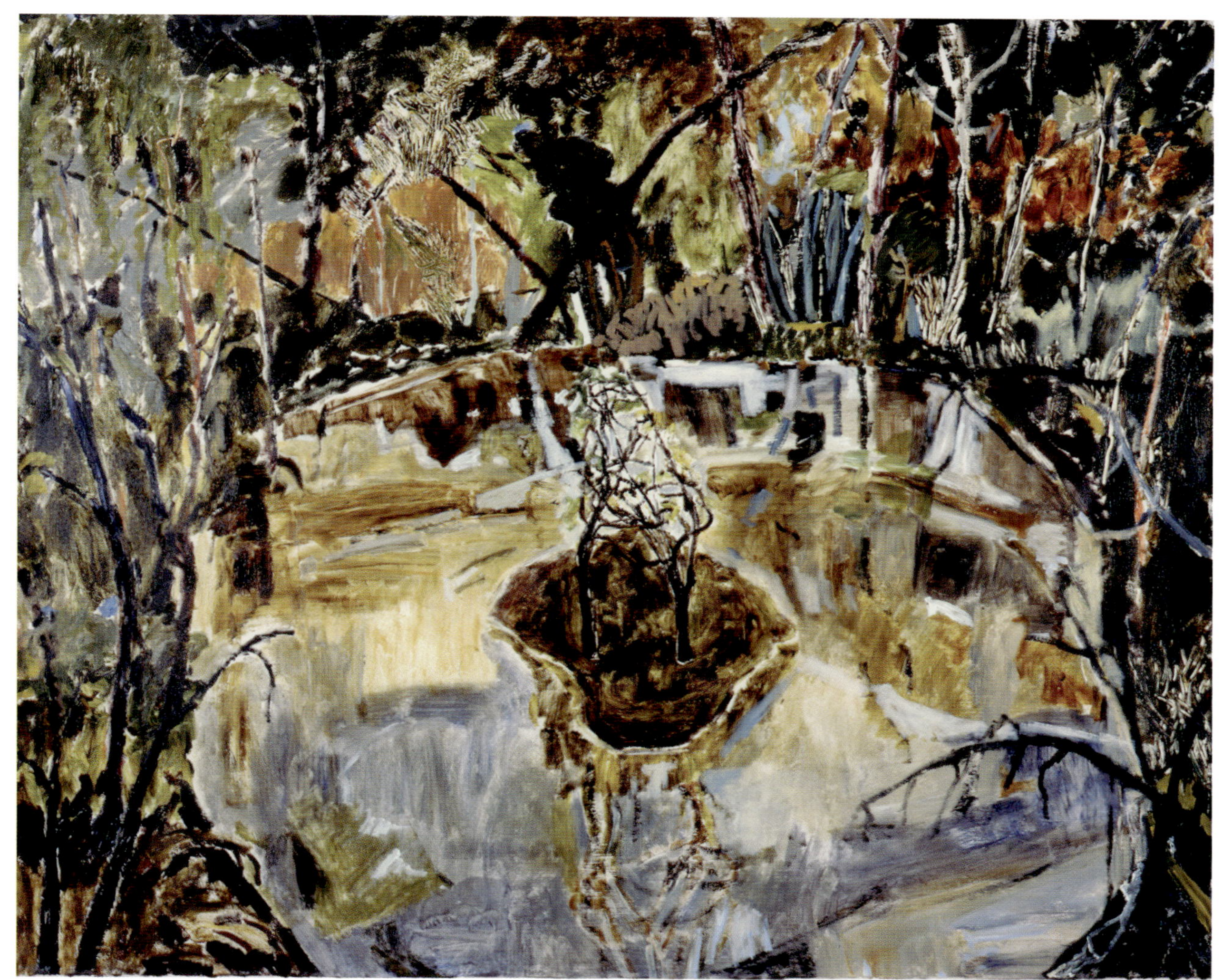

PLATE 4
Circle Island Duet, 1987, acrylic on canvas, 67.5 × 82 in.

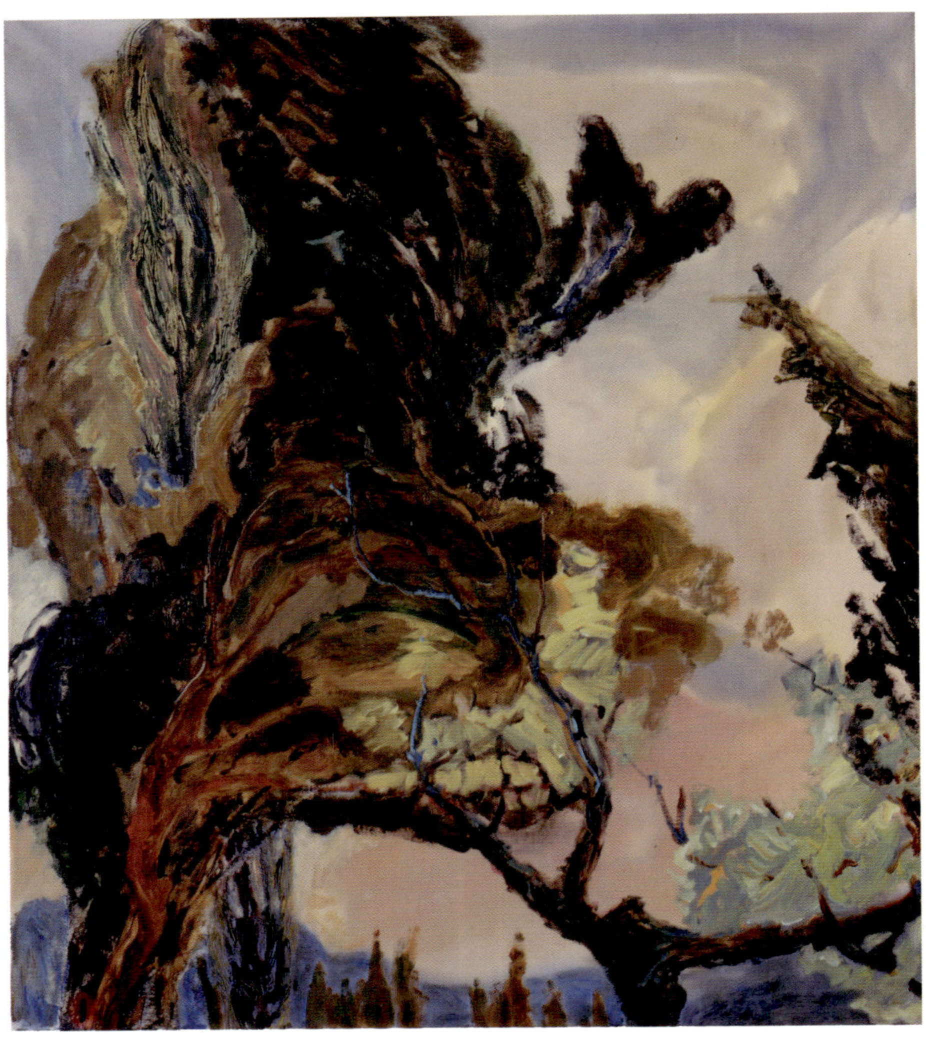

PLATE 5

Made to Bend, 1987, acrylic on canvas, 67.5 × 58 in.

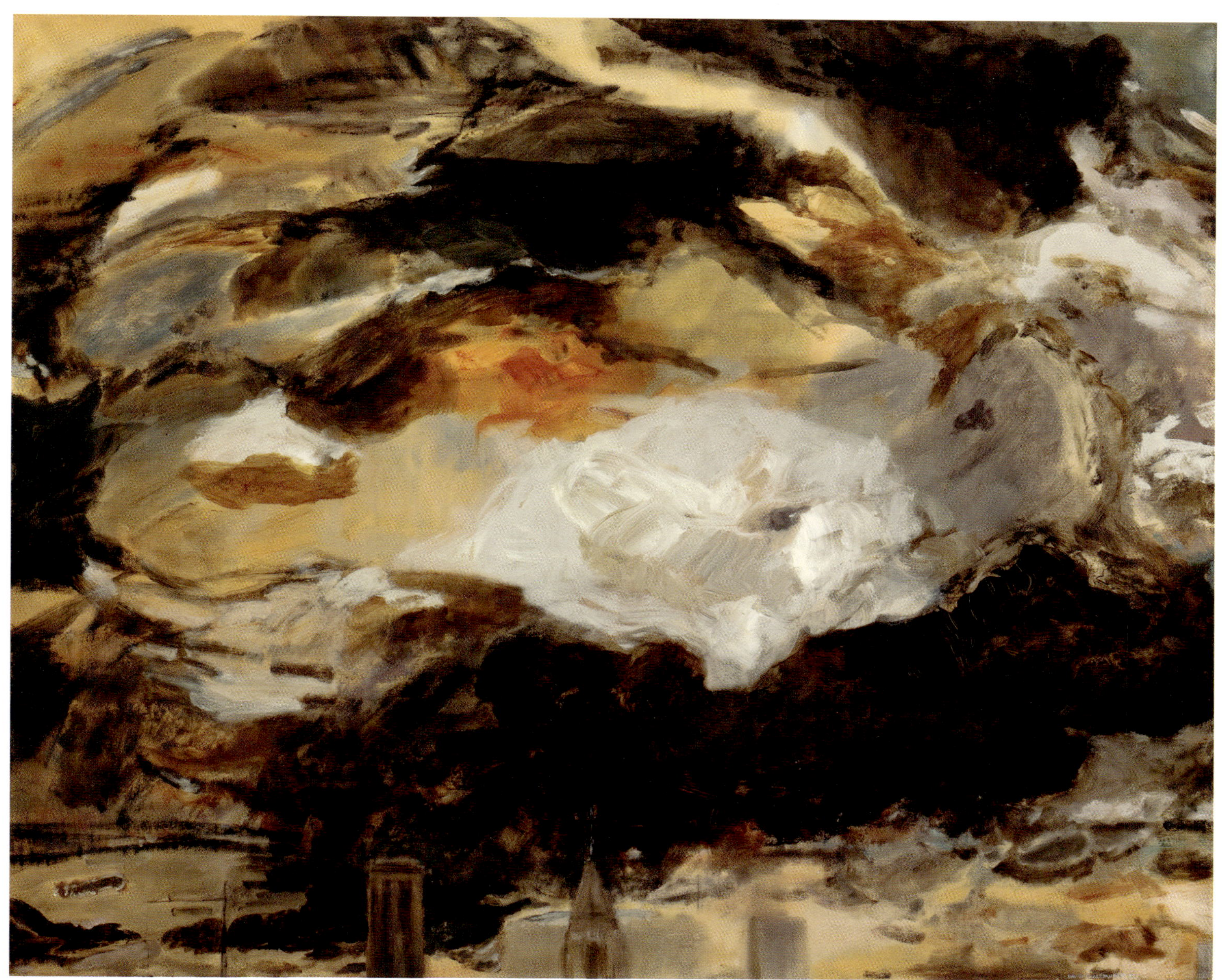

PLATE 6
The Tail End Surrounding, 1987, acrylic on canvas, 68 × 81 in.

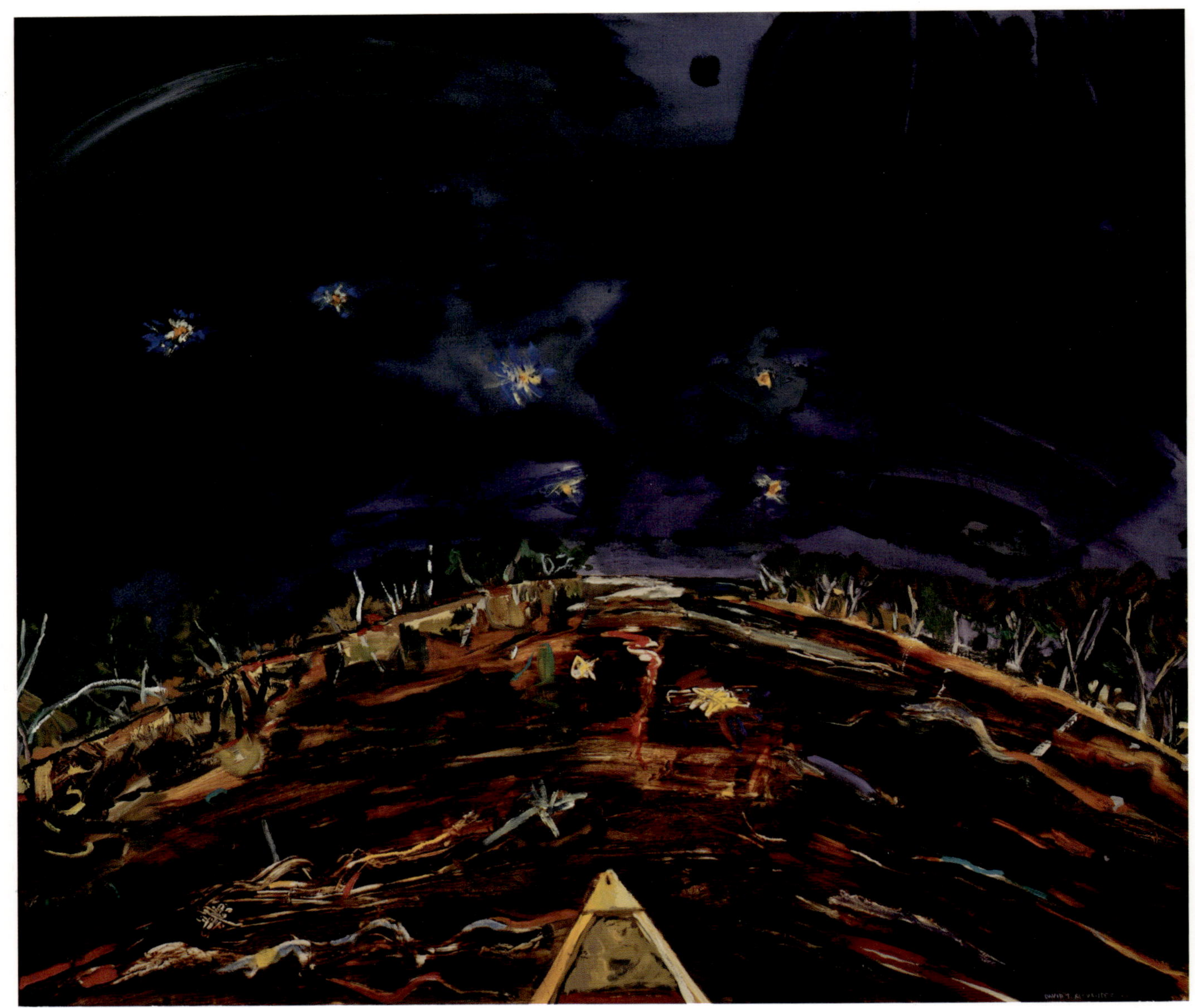

PLATE 7

Entering the Beginnings of the Big Dipper's Horizon, 1989, acrylic on canvas, 60 × 68 in.

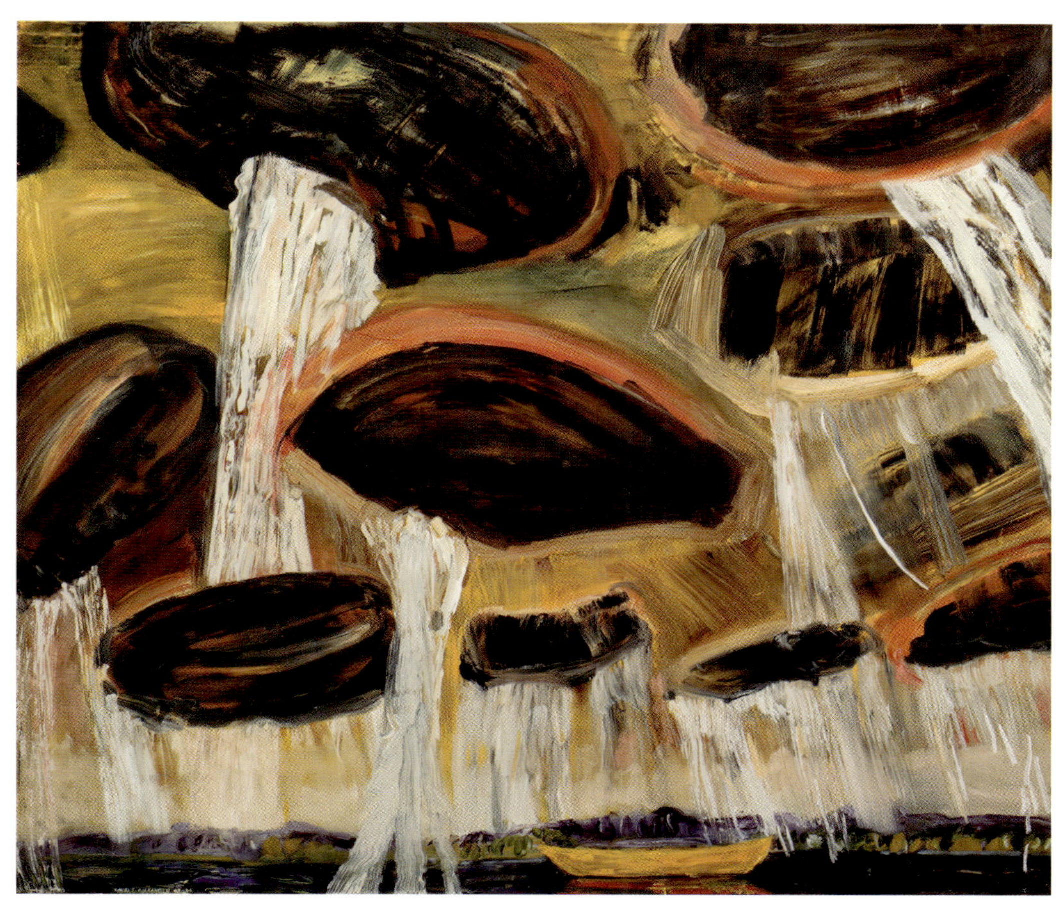

PLATE 8

Continuous Prairie Target Practice, 1989–94, acrylic on canvas, 58 × 67 in.

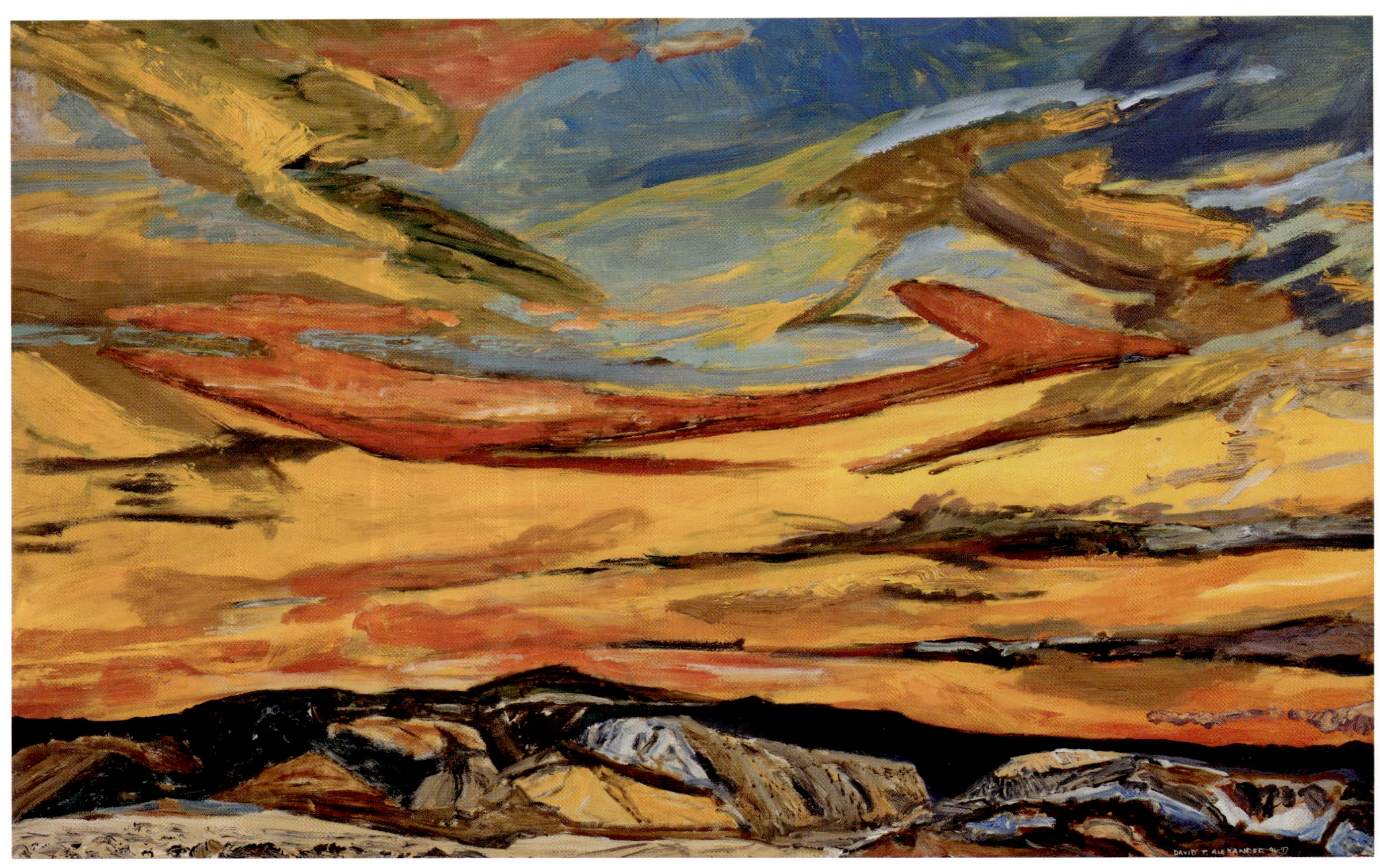

PLATE 9

Ellesmere Knife Clouds, 1996–97, acrylic on canvas, 57 × 90 in.

LANDSCAPE, NATURE: DAVID ALEXANDER

Sharon Butala

When I was asked to write this essay I responded that I write only personal essays and that I'm not a scholar, especially not about art. Although in the early sixties I had wanted to be a painter and had majored in art, I soon discovered I hadn't the talent or the drive necessary to live as an artist in Canada must live. "I discovered that I was probably going to want to eat," I told people when I went on to acquire a teaching degree. Since those days, what with marriage, motherhood, a teaching career, and as a writer living far out in the boonies, I had forgotten pretty much everything I ever knew about art. I lacked the language to talk about it, had only a half-forgotten fund of names, schools, paintings, painters, and their dates to call on. But, most intimidating of all, what we call art had changed drastically in the preceding forty years, and I had no framework in which to view it.

Still, my curiosity was aroused so before I refused, I looked up a number of David Alexander's recent paintings. It took me all of thirty seconds to fall in love with what I saw: the brilliant, clear colours, the originality, the – dare I say it? – the *beauty* of his work. I couldn't remember, glancing in gallery windows when I walked down a city street, or strolling casually through museums or civic galleries, ever having been so bowled over by contemporary paintings. I was no longer only mildly curious; I wanted something that translated, awkwardly and inaccurately, into knowing *how* he had done it. In the way of beauty lovers everywhere and through time, I wanted something other than mere possession-by-ownership. I wanted to stare until whatever that *other* is that humans so desire happened, something that would finally, somehow, close the gap between me and the object of beauty. I thought that if I couldn't respond as the knowledgeable art "consumer" or the serious critic, there had to be a way that I could be a part of this project, if only as someone who wanted to tell others about this artist's work, so that I too could celebrate his achievement.

It was apparent at once that Alexander and I do have some things in common: our love – almost a connoisseurship – of the much-denigrated Saskatchewan landscape, our common need to be in nature, and our practice of using nature as source and inspiration for our art. Possibly, I told myself, my sublime ignorance about contemporary art might not be so significant a handicap. Indeed, it might make it easier for me to focus on how his life and practice work together.

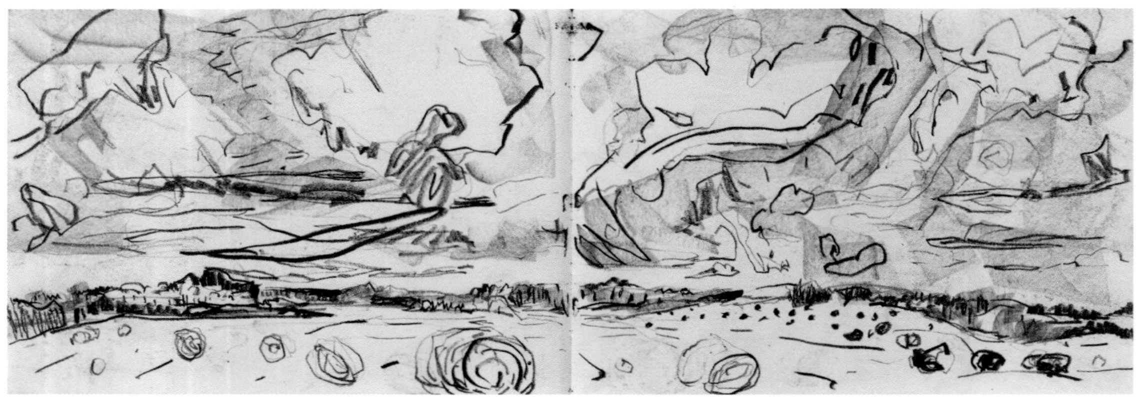

Untitled [Saskatchewan],
1990, graphite, 7.75 × 21.5 in.

I had been keen to meet him, although apprehensive, thinking nervously about the romantic notion of the male painter: morose, boorish, unkempt, monosyllabic, and, when it comes to domestic life, cagily, ruthlessly, uncommitted. But when David dropped in at my place and we spent an afternoon talking, he turned out to be none of the above, to such a degree that I had to laugh at my ideas, nourished as they were by a handful of famous examples: by Hollywood movies and the occasional novel. Intensely interested in the world, he seems not to sit so much as to perch, muscles tight, ready to move on should he spot something he needs to see. He told me a story about driving, his wife beside him, in the New Mexico desert, when suddenly he swerved off the road, bouncing along the rough ground at a high speed, intent on examining something he'd seen in the distance that couldn't wait. "I might have torn the bottom out of the car," he remarks, as if so what, that was the price to pay. His single-mindedness, I have to admit, does fit the stereotype. I was

moderately surprised to discover him also as a muscular, fit man, which seems to belong with his capacity for passionate engagement in most subjects, his great and (I thought) unusual excitement at the world, and his endless curiosity. He is verbal and very articulate, characteristics I hadn't expected. With so active a mind at work in this equally active body, there seemed to be no room for untoward vanity, and no time for the posturing that so alienates the public from the "artiste" when it doesn't amuse them. He seemed to me at once more athletic and more fun to be around than my preconception of the male artist would allow.

He told me that he was just about to celebrate his fortieth wedding anniversary and had dropped in to see me on his way from visiting one of his two children who, despite having been born into a family where the father was never anything but an artist, seemed to have turned out more than passably well. Forty years of a single, happy marriage here in the twenty-first century, as I hardly need emphasize, is increasingly rare. And finally, there doesn't appear to have ever been the proverbial garret in his life – the one I was afraid of enough to transfer out of art – although as a young husband and father he doubtless had some lean times. Currently (David is in his early sixties), he and Judy live in a large, modern house they designed with their builder, set into a hillside overlooking Okanagan Lake. David, at last successful enough to afford the dream house, and confident enough with himself and his art to be able to go home, nonetheless chose Kelowna rather than Nelson or Vancouver because it was one place in BC they had never lived. If I was surprised by all of this, I was also satisfied, having refused to accept all my writer's life what I saw as the male pose – sometimes it isn't a pose – of the unreliable, two-fisted, drinking womanizer as the only place out of which art can come. Or the reclusive ascetic. Both of them extremes, when I suspect that through the ages the great bulk of artists – the great ones, too – led relatively "normal" lives, except when forced into exile by their work or imprisoned for it. It is a great curiosity about the world, combined with single-mindedness, that make the artist: I think of Shakespeare, the greatest of them all, who was an insatiable omnivore when it came to the world.

As a writer I am also principally interested in what makes people tick, and after learning all of this in the first half-hour of meeting him, I then wondered what the wellspring of David's art might be. I remarked to him that art – according to current psychotherapeutic notions – often seems to come out of some great childhood wound borne by the artist: violence, abuse, neglect. But he was having none of that, and disagreed politely with the notion, shrugging off the idea as it

related to himself and saying firmly that he didn't believe that such wounding would always produce an artist. He told me a little about his childhood, which, I had to agree, seemed as normal as most Canadian childhoods. When he was a child, the family spent every summer on Gambier Island off Horseshoe Bay, near Vancouver. From a young age, he was accustomed to going up and down the coast on his father's tugboat and worked on the boat for a number of summers as a teenager. Enough time to get to know water better than most of us and, whether he was consciously aware of this or not, to become aware of the mystery of water – its shapes and forms, how its surface changes and changes again, never stops changing. He remarks that viewing the coast as the boat went slowly past gave him the opportunity, time and again, to study the coastal landscape.

He had the good luck to be born into a household that accepted the making of art: both his mother and his grandmother were artists. Emily Carr was a neighbour of his mother's in Victoria; as a child she went with a friend to Carr's house for tea every Sunday. Consequently, she made a point of introducing David to Carr's work when he was still very young. Probably as a result of this, he is unable to date the time when he first thought of himself as an artist; although he offers around grade five or six as a possibility, he seems to have taken that designation from the first as something of a given. By the time he was fourteen he had his own studio, although he says he never thought of it as such. When his older brother left home, David was allowed to use the room and to put all his "stuff" into it; he had been making art for a long time by then. He apparently considered no other career, no other way

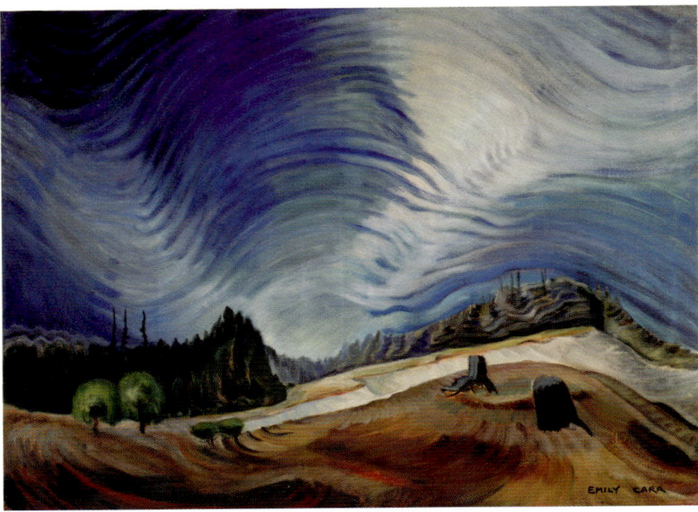

Emily Carr, *Above the Gravel Pit*, 1937,
oil on canvas, 30.4 × 40.3 in.
Collection of the Vancouver Art Gallery.

of life (although, of course, he worked at other jobs to support himself and, eventually, his family). His focus in high school was always on art as the one place where he could feel himself to be successful, the one subject that always gave him the most profound satisfaction. It was also the place where he found his first art teacher. In subsequent years, she continued to follow David's progress, even brought him a bottle of Courvoisier to celebrate the opening of his first major show, though she also always brought a severe critical eye to his work as well.

After high school, he attended the Langara Campus of the Vancouver Community College (1971–72), and in 1978 received a BFA from Notre Dame University in Nelson, BC. During that time in Nelson he worked virtually alone for several years, he says, painting the British Columbia landscape. In 1979, Anthony Emery, then a past director of the

Vancouver Art Gallery, showed an interest in David's work and suggested to him that he could use some new stimulation. In response, David cast about for a workshop to attend outside BC, and found one that appealed to him – "I picked it because I liked the name," he says, amused at the way he had unwittingly chosen the place that would be perhaps the biggest influence on his life as an artist. He headed off for two weeks to the Emma Lake Artists' Workshop in forested central Saskatchewan near Prince Albert, a small city that bills itself, and has ever since I can remember, as "the gateway to the North."

The art school at Murray Point on Emma Lake had been founded in 1930 by the landscape painter Augustus Kenderdine; in 1939, it became a campus of the University of Saskatchewan.[1] The much-loved landscape and figure painter and teacher, Ernest Lindner (who was my high school art teacher in the fifties and whose influence in the Saskatchewan art community cannot be underestimated), had for many years owned – and spent his summers at – a cabin on a small island just yards from the Emma Lake campus. David's arrival occurred at a time when artists were coming by the dozens. The school was flourishing and the social life and sense of freedom artists found there were compelling and invigorating. From the 1960s on, the Emma Lake art school was the place to be during the summer.

In Saskatchewan, David says, he found a community of artists who supported one another, who knew one another's work intimately, and discussed it freely, intensely, and in a spirit of inquiry: what worked and what didn't, why or why not, what other avenues might be open to achieve an effect. Argument, discussion, laughter – all were characteristic of the school at that time, and the artists David met there accepted him without preliminaries or caveats. He told me of that experience, "I received more feedback in two weeks than I had in eight years" (another reason that the university was wrong when, a few years ago, it was making noises about closing down the school).

He went back to Nelson and his wife Judy, he says, saw at once that something profound had happened. They talked it over, and eventually she asked, "Do you want to move there?" He didn't hesitate. "Yes," he said. They had two small children and no jobs, but in 1980 they packed and left Nelson for Saskatoon, intending to stay two years. "We stayed twenty-three," he said. "Home" is perhaps too cozy, too closed a

word, to describe what he felt in the art community at Emma Lake and then in Saskatoon. At the University of Saskatchewan, where he enrolled in the Master's degree program in 1980, he wrote his thesis, fittingly, on the work of Claude Monet and was also required to mount an exhibition of his own work to obtain the degree.

In the 1980s, Saskatchewan was one of the country's hot spots for making art, talking about it, and studying it. In 1961, the Regina Five had made their initial impression across the country, calling national attention to the province as a place where exciting art was being made. In Saskatchewan, for the first time in his artist's life, Alexander says he was truly inspired. His excitement was explosive, a result of all the open engagement and supportive stimulation he received and an atmosphere in which competition and overriding ambition, though present, added to the exhilaration rather than destroying would-be artists.

Besides this turbulent atmosphere, or maybe in part because of it, critics and artists were coming from all over the English-speaking world to Emma Lake and to Saskatoon. Clement Greenberg was a frequent visitor, as was the New York abstract painter (also a sculptor, print-maker, and maker of drawings) Stanley Boxer. The latter came to Saskatchewan many times, David told me, and he refers to him as a mentor: "He had things to say that hurt or were wonderful." Often, other painters got no feedback from Boxer, but he gave Alexander much that was useful to him in terms of his art. Boxer so energized him that he returned to see him in New York several times. David speaks of the "liberty of it all," and how, in Saskatoon, he learned to be "out of control, whereas in Vancouver things were too controlled." He began to make brave art, crossing boundaries, heedless of standards, following his own impulses, not trying to stifle them in case they might lead to a mistake or dead end.

During the years David was studying, he also often broke the rhythm of life in the studio and university by travelling on his own to New York, London, Paris, and Holland to do research, to see what was going on in the art world. He told me that in his years working around Nelson, he saw no paintings of the sort the art world was talking about, or by the masters: to see such works had to have been moving, instructive, and enlightening. He also made several trips to Giverny to see Monet's home, garden, and the pond he so famously painted. He says of those visits that they "… made me realize that his genius was beyond the pictorial scene and was very intimate in scope. I think that became my focus. I began to zero in on complexity but in very short space."[2] In a 1994 interview with curator Dan Ring at Saskatoon's Mendel Gallery, he said, "But that sense of surface was important to me early on, a part of my consideration of Monet which has influenced my work, for example, *Eastbank to Pike* [1985]. Instead of dealing with the reality of what's above you, you deal with the reality of what you're looking at, which is a fractured surface in turmoil, which also fractures your nature, your sense of self."[3]

After David and his family arrived in Saskatoon, he began the long process of adjusting to a landscape that was the antithesis of the one he had grown up in and been painting for years, with its mountains, pine and spruce forests, cascading waterfalls, rushing, tumultuous mountain streams, and

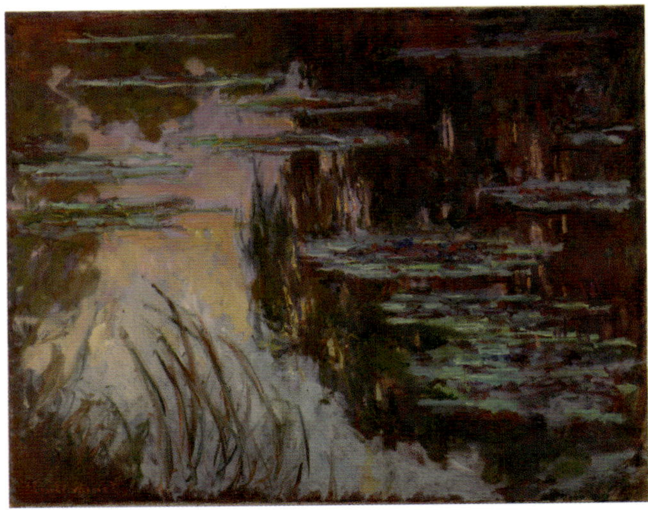

Claude Monet, *Water-Lilies, Setting Sun*, about 1907, oil on canvas, 28.7 × 36.5 in. © National Gallery, London / Art Resource, NY.

mysterious, infinite ocean. When he speaks of the transformation that occurred in his life as an artist over the years in Saskatchewan, he doesn't speak so much of adjusting to the deciduous trees and rolling grassland of Saskatchewan's parklands that surround the city of Saskatoon, as he does about "learning to look." In visual terms, in artistic terms, he says, the move into this vastly different landscape forced him to learn to look all over again, to look in a different way. His progress as a painter of landscapes came out of the advances he made in learning to look; it was mostly in Saskatchewan that he made these leaps. He had come with all that "BC baggage." "I moved here in 1980," he says, "and my brain came in 1989." It came to him suddenly that "the prairie is about sky – ever-changing, unpredictable, the stimulant of powerful emotions."

It was there, in the midst of tremendous excitement, that his vision, his desire, and his sense of untapped possibilities for his art began to grow. One day around the year 2000, out in the Redberry-Blaine Lake area looking for something to paint with Tim Nowlin, painter, friend, and University of Saskatchewan professor of art, they came upon a small slough. It was late evening David says, with a very light wind blowing and a yellow filtered light low on the horizon. The slough was rimmed by the usual shrubs – willows, probably saskatoons and chokecherry bushes – and tall slough grasses; the water was darkish, its surface strewn here and there with bits of floating vegetation. There was, in itself, nothing unusual about it. But as the two men walked and looked, they saw colour which began to intensify, to deepen, even as it changed location and shape, to move and flow and grow richer as they watched the water intently. "Look, look," David kept saying to Nowlin, who ran back and forth, excitedly snapping photos. David mimed his excitement as he tried to help me understand what had happened to him, and I began to grasp the nature of the experience, to feel his excitement and awe at what he had been fortunate enough to see – or more accurately, what he had experienced. "It just kept getting better and better and better," he said, his eyes fixed on the memory. "I couldn't believe that it could get better." And after a moment, still not looking at me, "And then, bang, it was over. Like a clap of thunder."

I tried to understand what had happened, thinking in terms of expanded consciousness and of a transcendental experience in nature. Yet Alexander didn't say that, and it is hard to imagine two people experiencing such a thing at the same time.

I began to think that he was talking about something only painters, trained and alert enough to the visual, could have fully grasped. Perhaps it is superfluous to speak of the transcendental, although those of us without the artist's eye could have failed to understand the importance of what David and Tim Nowlin saw that day. "Nice," we might have said, scraping a little mud off a boot, taking a bite out of a sandwich.

It would be difficult to exaggerate the experience's significance to him. "I could have put my whole life's work in that half hour," he told me, adding that his whole *Wet* series, remarkable pictures of great beauty and depth, in which he has been immersed for about ten years, probably began with that moment. It was about the wonder of the world, about its possibilities, and the *Wet* series seems to this writer to be about the constant change of the world in process. He also remarked to me that maybe that experience was what made it possible for him to leave Saskatchewan.

I have said that we had in common our love of nature and our use of nature as inspiration and subject for our art. But when I sat down with David and broached the subject of what nature means to him, at first I got no answers that satisfied me. Because he is an articulate man, I was surprised. Was I asking the wrong questions? How might a painter and a writer who both take nature as their subject speak to one another of the way the landscape influences a life, changes one's view? How it teaches? How it inspires? All the question needed, it turns out, was a more – pardon the pun – down-to-earth approach.

David told me that he has spent most of his life out in the countryside, even when his home was in cities: Vancouver,

Nelson, Saskatoon. He is intimately familiar with the land-scapes he paints, and is a capable and fit outdoorsman, hiker, and camper, unafraid of going alone into the wilderness for relatively long periods in search of pictures to paint. As an older woman, a non-athlete, and a cattle rancher's wife for more than thirty years (nature isn't recreation to us, it is how we make a living, though this could also be said of the land-scape painter), I was bound to have a different approach to nature. When I was not outside helping my husband with ranch jobs, I used nature as solace and as a quiet place for contemplation. In nature, I slowed down and if I did not hike, climb, or swim, collect rocks, or name birds and flowers, or paint or sketch on such treks, I did make a practice of looking hard at things. At such times I wanted only to be in nature. If I was still and quiet enough, if I was empty, and saw myself as less than nature, (not in control of it, or seeking to be), I knew that I would make a connection with the natural world as a presence or a consciousness.

Mine was a directly spiritual quest: I was trying to know nature so well, to see so deeply into it, that I might catch a glimpse of the fabric of which the universe is made and begin to understand the human capacity for knowing a world greater than the material one. Or, it might be said, trying to find the lost or forgotten human capacity for knowing nature. David's approach is more adventurous and daring than mine and it is a more active search. Even within the context of our very different approaches, he began to say things with which I could connect. He spoke of "letting go of the self and being a part of it, and that part is visually the sun, the grass, all those things we haven't tried to 'culturize.'" I remarked that if you tried to talk about nature as spirit, "people think you are a moron." David responded "I know I'm not a moron when I'm in nature."

Once I'd thought about it, I realized I didn't know what he meant by that remark, and wrote to him to ask for an ex-planation. He wrote back that "When I am engrossed in the experience of nature I am totally involved in where and what I am doing in that eventful minute/hour/week, etc., and that makes the thoughts strong enough for me to create from the gathered information. The cerebral takes a holiday for a bit." And further on, "I don't know all the reasons I go into nature other than that I know I am not judged, rejected, or congrat-ulated for being there. I just feel good."[4]

I have always believed that nature responds to human emo-tion and to human purpose if – a big "if" – one rids oneself of the ego when present in it, if one stops thinking, as David says he does, and if one allows awe, the awe that is the natural human response to nature, all the space it needs. Then nature opens up, shows one things that others don't see, lets one see beyond the trees, grass, flowers, rocks, to the fabric of which it is made. Call it what you will, just don't think you know it, because then you will never see anything.

Perhaps David's fascination with Simon Schama's book *Landscape and Memory* is a part of this looking. Schama points out that every landscape has a history, usually a human his-tory, and that we don't look at nature with clear eyes, but with a culturally-conditioned mindset. David says of Schama, "he helped me understand that there are thousands of ways we come to the nature of land and what we add to the knowledge is only bits and pieces, but it does make me think, research, and try to understand the use, abuse, and reconstitution of nature." He goes on to say that is the reason why going to land that is less familiar to us, less "touched" land such as the high Arctic, is so important to him. Such places offer an insight into land and a sense of place that he might not otherwise find. Places that are intensely used and familiar are hard to see, he points out, and the question of the relationship between culture and nature continues to absorb him.

He spoke, for example, about a hiking trip he went on in 1988 across Ellesmere Island. After hours of walking in company across the tundra, he grew so bored with the hike that, without realizing it, he began to study the ground as he walked across it, seeing the tussocks of grass and the places where the permafrost had melted away. He got so that without looking he could tell the noise of someone stepping on a tussock, a sound that stays with him to this day. If it had at first seemed to me that we were trying to connect about nature from two different perspectives, I was beginning to see that in the intensity of looking, losing oneself in physical details, becoming a part of the experience rather than merely an observer of it, he and I understood each other perfectly. It was in doing the research for this essay that I discovered something of which I had been only vaguely aware: the disrepute that painting had fallen into in the 1980s and that to try to become a recognized artist as a landscape painter was to be relegated to the "dustbin of history," as the saying goes. Alexander, however, seems to have had no difficulty at all in resisting the pressure to change paths. Without apology he has remained a painter, and a landscape painter at that. I imagine this is so, at least in part, because of the life-long intensity of his relationship to nature.

He does, laughingly, refer to himself as a "dinosaur," with something approaching pride in his voice, pride in having stuck to the path he chose in the face of discouragement and in having been proven right at last. Interestingly though, so closely does he examine the landscape that his paintings almost dissolve into the non-representational. Almost, but not. In all his work I was able to identify the features of the natural world that inspired it. It seems to me simply extraordinary that he is able to keep painting in this way, and to experience little or no conflict about doing it, nor any real sense that there might be a limit to his ability or process. Extraordinary that his drive as an artist pushes him to look so deeply that he sees things it seems no one else has seen. Never mind his "debt" to the Fauves, or as some critics have said, to Tom Thomson. David, in fact, sees the Group of Seven as a presence with which every Canadian landscape painter has to come to terms. Because he is a West Coast painter, the same is true of the influence of Emily Carr; he even called a forest painting of his *Emily, You're Almost Off My Back* (1986–87). His deep interest in the work of Claude Monet can also be read as indicative of his search for the fresh place out of which he might paint landscape.

This search for a new perspective is part of the reason Alexander spends so much time in nature. And it is how he makes the landscape new and wonderful all over again. It is as if through hard, experienced, and informed vision he has seen that the world is not fact but process, and it is the process that he paints. He wanted to be part of a Mount Everest expedition because his eyes might have been opened even wider to let him see how the world is made. Viewed from this perspective, I see how huge the disappointment must have been when the trip didn't happen.

His excitement at going to spend three weeks working in the Grand Canyon in June of 2010 was palpable. From a couple of erratic, truncated emails, and a cell phone call that kept breaking up, I felt he wasn't so much driving there as flying, propelled by excitement. To see things no one has seen before, to see as the Impressionists saw, some other way of looking at the world. For them, it was looking at light and shadow on the surface of things, as if for the first time, when they moved out into *plein air* to paint directly from nature. For Alexander, it is looking at the natural world in motion, creating itself. It was thrilling to be near such excitement, such hope. I wondered how he had managed to maintain this excitement for the many years of his life as a painter. It could only be, I thought, because of his growing sense that he was making progress in understanding how the world is made. Out of all of this – his love of nature, his avidity for it, his fearlessness – come his landscapes: muscular, dramatic, with an edge of something close to violence, conveying a deep sense of nature's power.

I started this essay by saying that I was so attracted to his work because it struck me simply as very beautiful. I also said that I didn't know the first thing about art. I wonder, though, what is "the first thing about art"? I, along with most of the viewing public, would once have said "beauty"without hesitation. But beauty as a singular objective in art bit the dust a long time ago, and yet it seems that many artists keep on producing it, whether by accident or design, and the viewing public still responds to it, pretty much above all else. As I was so attracted to David's work because I found it so beautiful, and given the troubled history of beauty in contemporary art, I finally thought to ask him if he consciously tried to create beauty when he painted a picture. After musing a while, he responded that he supposed he did try to create beauty, but "it's not important to me if a picture is beautiful, but a plus if it is recognized to be so."

It was colour in his work I fell in love with as much as anything else. It is another thing we hold in common, this tremendous love for the colour in the world. What is unusual is that he found such amazing colour in the prairie landscape too, a pure turquoise line in water, a shifting patch of lemon yellow, or orange or red, as if he had taken the blankness of abstract art's colour and put it to use again. He says, in an interview with Robert Enright: "The colours I use might only happen for a fraction of a second as a reflection, or it might be the rock reflecting the light, but it's all there. So I exaggerate within my own colour sense."[5]

So, when I first looked at David's paintings, I fell for the colour, the beauty. As I looked a little longer, I also became fascinated by the movement in the painted landscapes: his expression of struggle inside a landscape, of its own sense of incompleteness. Maybe that's David's sense, as if soon things would come together; something would appear out of the landscape that would explain everything. Or the sense of the on-going struggle of something to appear, whatever it was. Nothing finished, but in calm equilibrium, waiting only for us to admire it. I thought I recognized something that I too have always thought about nature: the huge sense of power inherent in landscape, hovering just below the surface of what we look at and experience. Sometimes I think that for all the brilliance of colour, David sees menace everywhere. Mystery and menace.

Clement Greenberg wrote that, "Art is – among other things – continuity, and unthinkable without it."[6] So just where does Alexander fit into the continuity of landscape painting? As a young Canadian painter he had no choice but to think about the work of the Group of Seven and Tom Thomson. As a graduate student he studied Monet, and then later was excited by the work of David Milne, in particular, he says, about the possibilities of the use of line in painting. The radical shift from the rugged and dangerous mountain land-scape of British Columbia to the relatively spare, minimalist Saskatchewan landscape taught him to look all over again, and in looking, he saw the sky, and then he saw the water. Unlike Monet, he began to paint something deeper – his interpreta-tion of the natural world, how it is alive and constantly in motion, no matter how still the day, how clear the light. He doesn't paint scenic vistas, but enters the landscape and paints its immediacy. In doing so, he has carried on the landscape painting tradition, but has found a way to both signify and remain within the recognizable world, and to see into it more

deeply than other artists. Fearing the trap of nostalgia and its untruth above all else, this is a painter who opened his eyes so wide that they changed the world. He didn't then stultify in that vision, didn't let it solidify, but let it be a mode, a process, so that as long as the world remains in flux, the wonder never stops. What I see in his work, in a word, is *joy*.

NOTES

1 Keith Bell, "Claiming Saskatchewan: Landscape Painting from 1905 to 1950," in *Perspectives of Saskatchewan*, ed. Jene M. Porter (Winnipeg: University of Manitoba Press, 2009), 264.

2 David Alexander, email message to the author, 6 July 2010.

3 Dan Ring, *David Alexander* (Saskatoon: Mendel Art Gallery, 1995), 25.

4 David Alexander, email message to the author, 4 July 2010.

5 Robert Enright, "The Pride of Influence: A Conversation with David Alexander," *Border Crossings* 4, no. 3 (Summer 1997): 60.

6 Clement Greenberg, *The Collected Essays and Criticism: Modernism with a Vengeance, 1957–1969*, ed. John O'Brian (Chicago: University of Chicago Press, 1993), 93.

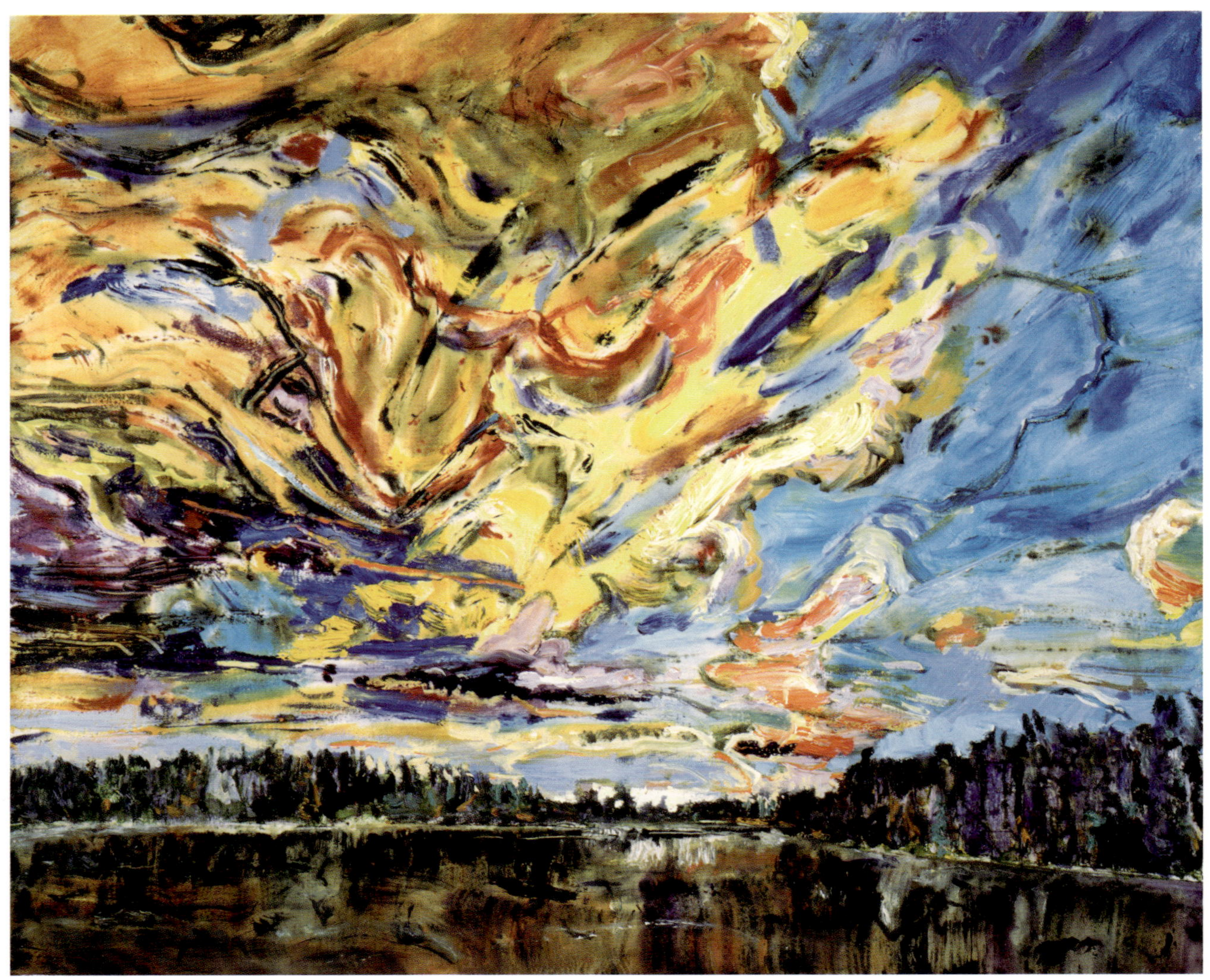

Visual Music for Ozzie, 1992, acrylic on canvas, 60 × 68 in.

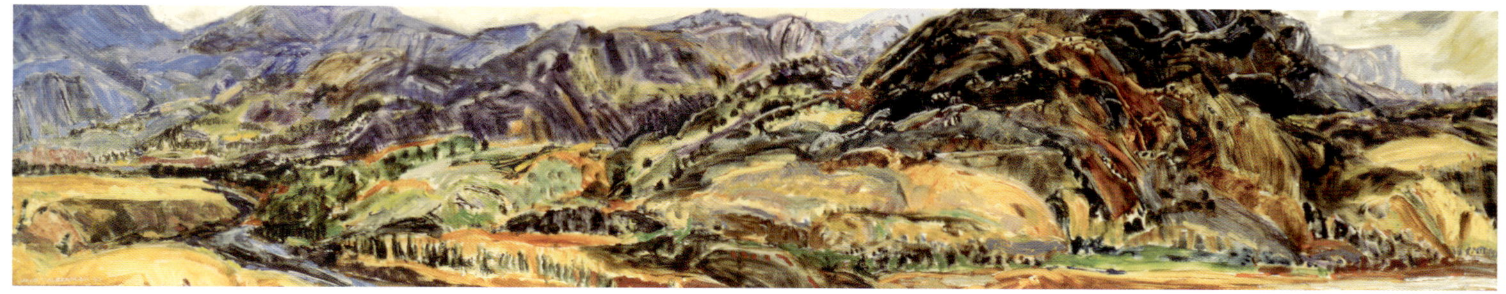

Winding through the Vault, 1992, acrylic on canvas, 24 × 118 in.

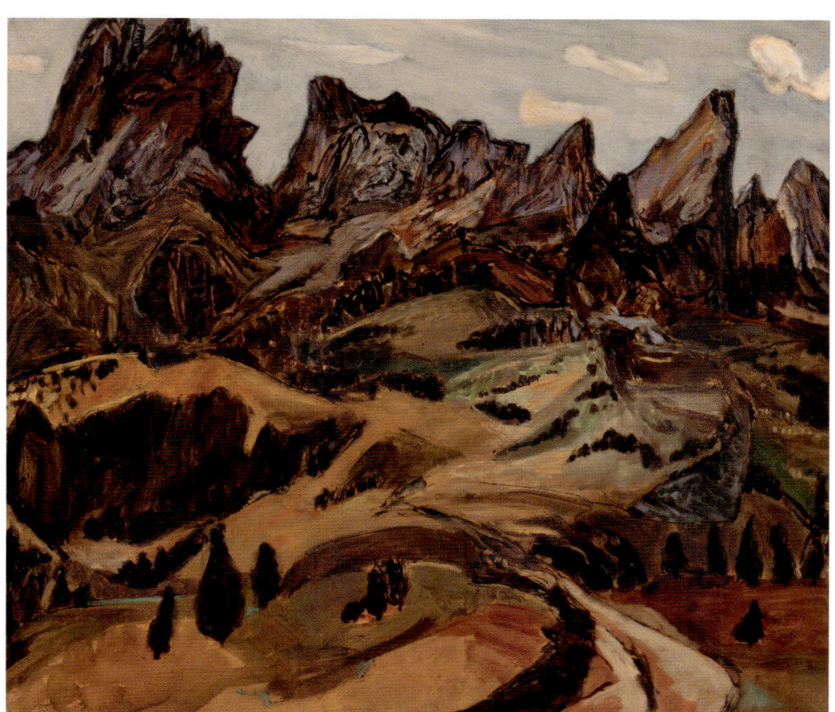

Higher Gargoyles, 1994, acrylic
on canvas, 60 × 66 in.

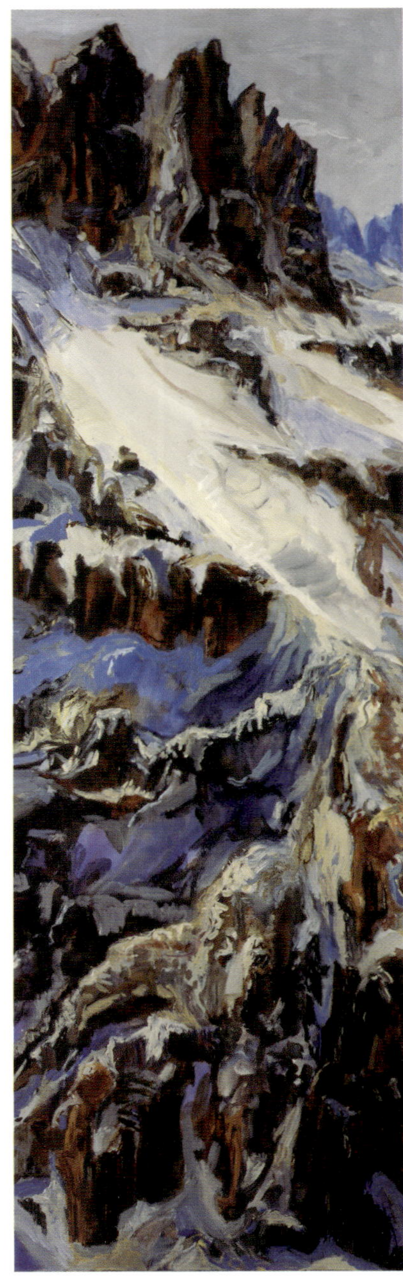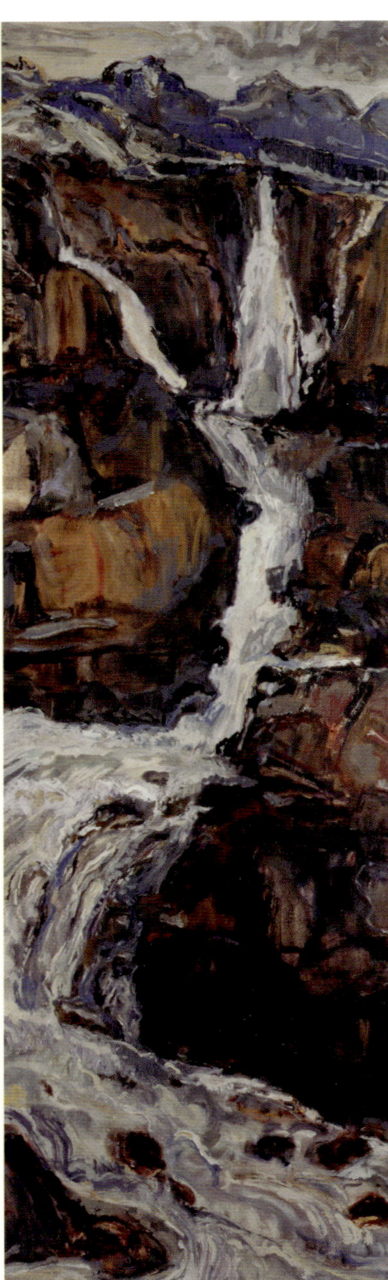

PLATE 13   Left
Silence Triumphs from the Prophetic Sawtooth Spine, 1996, acrylic on canvas, 78 × 23 in.

PLATE 14   Right
Silent Patience Among the Plumed Towers, 1996, acrylic on canvas, 95 × 23 in.

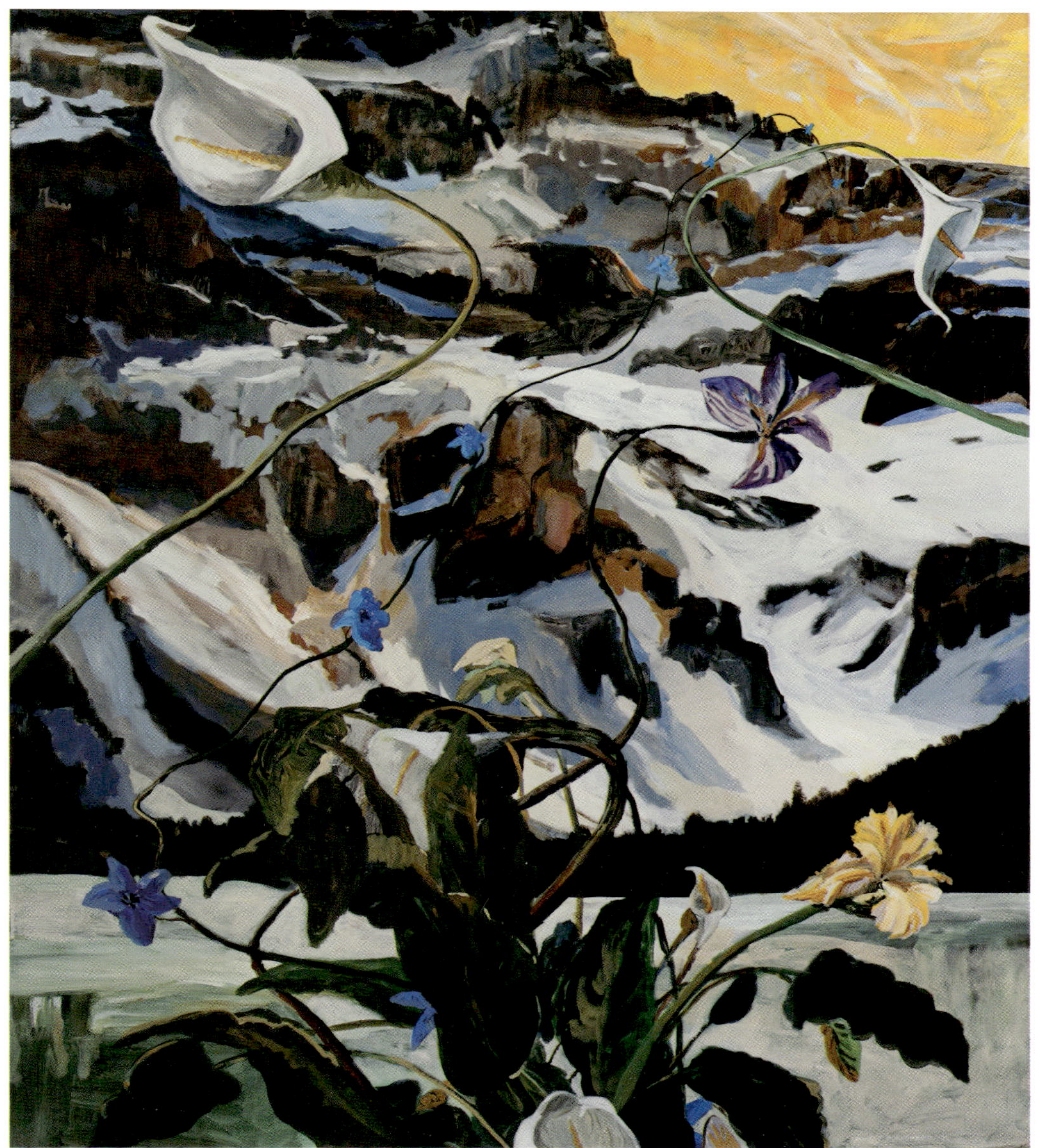

Place of Domestication, 1998, acrylic on canvas, 67 × 58 in.

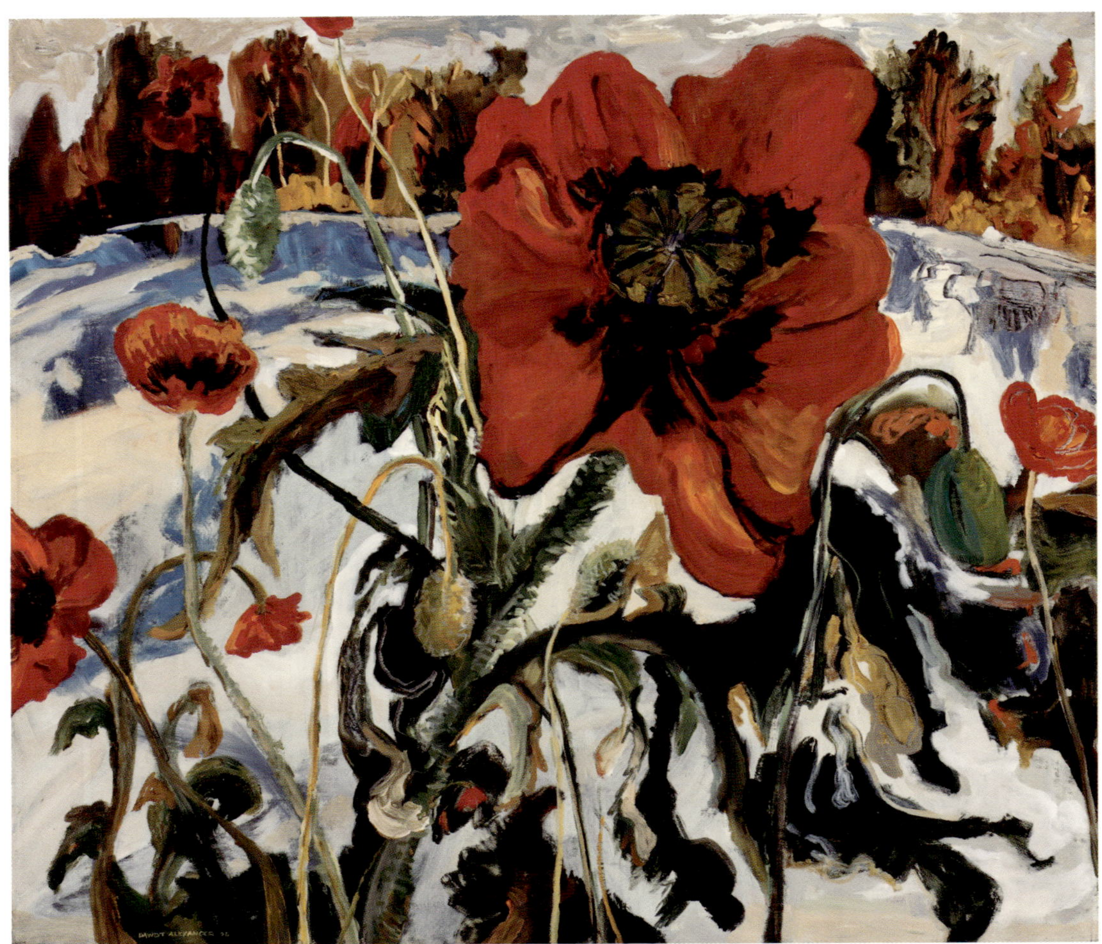

PLATE 16

Reds over a Northern Winter, 1998, acrylic on canvas, 57.5 × 66 in.

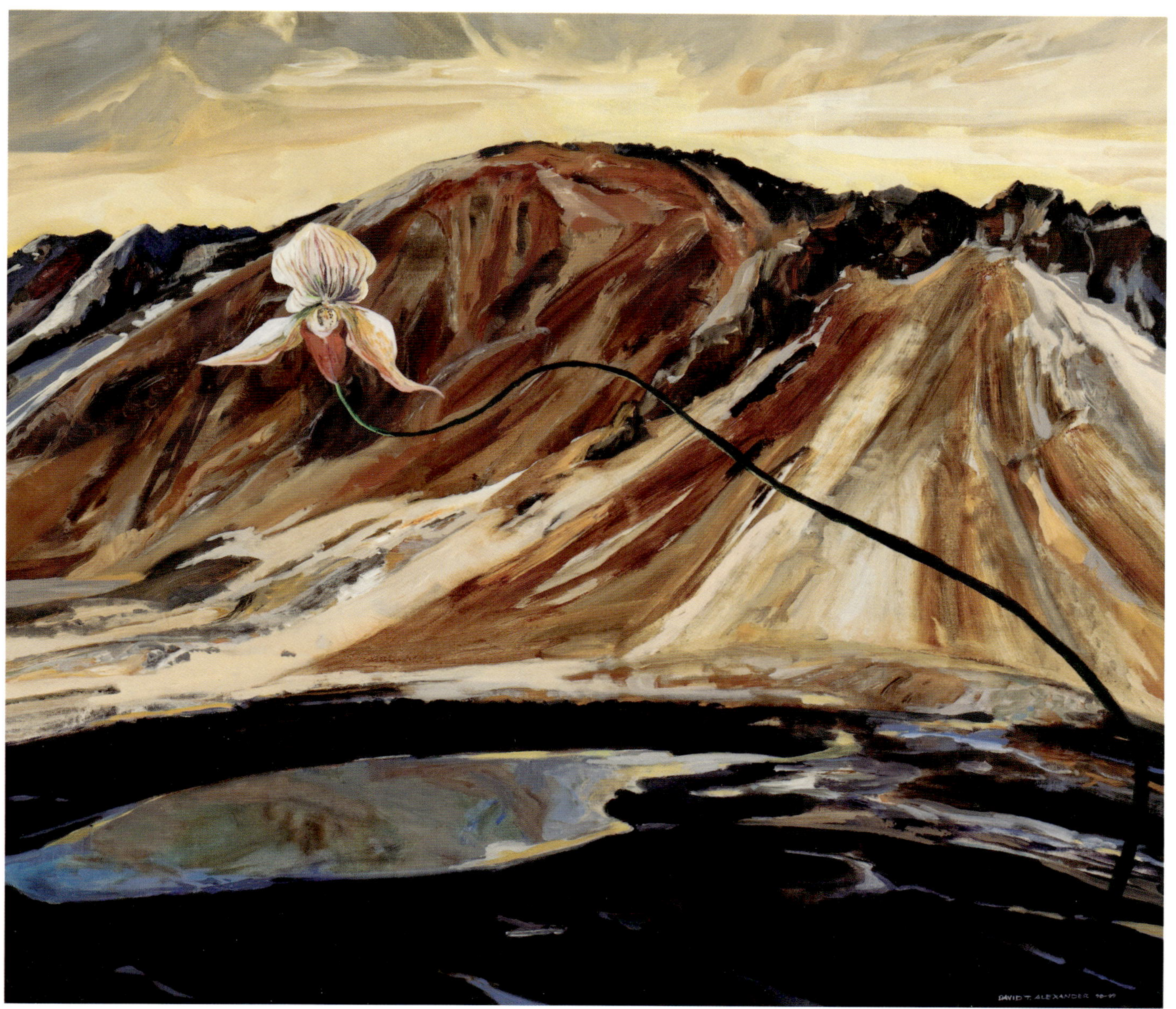

PLATE 17

Not Much Belongs in the Arctic, 1998–99, acrylic on canvas, 58.5 × 68 in.

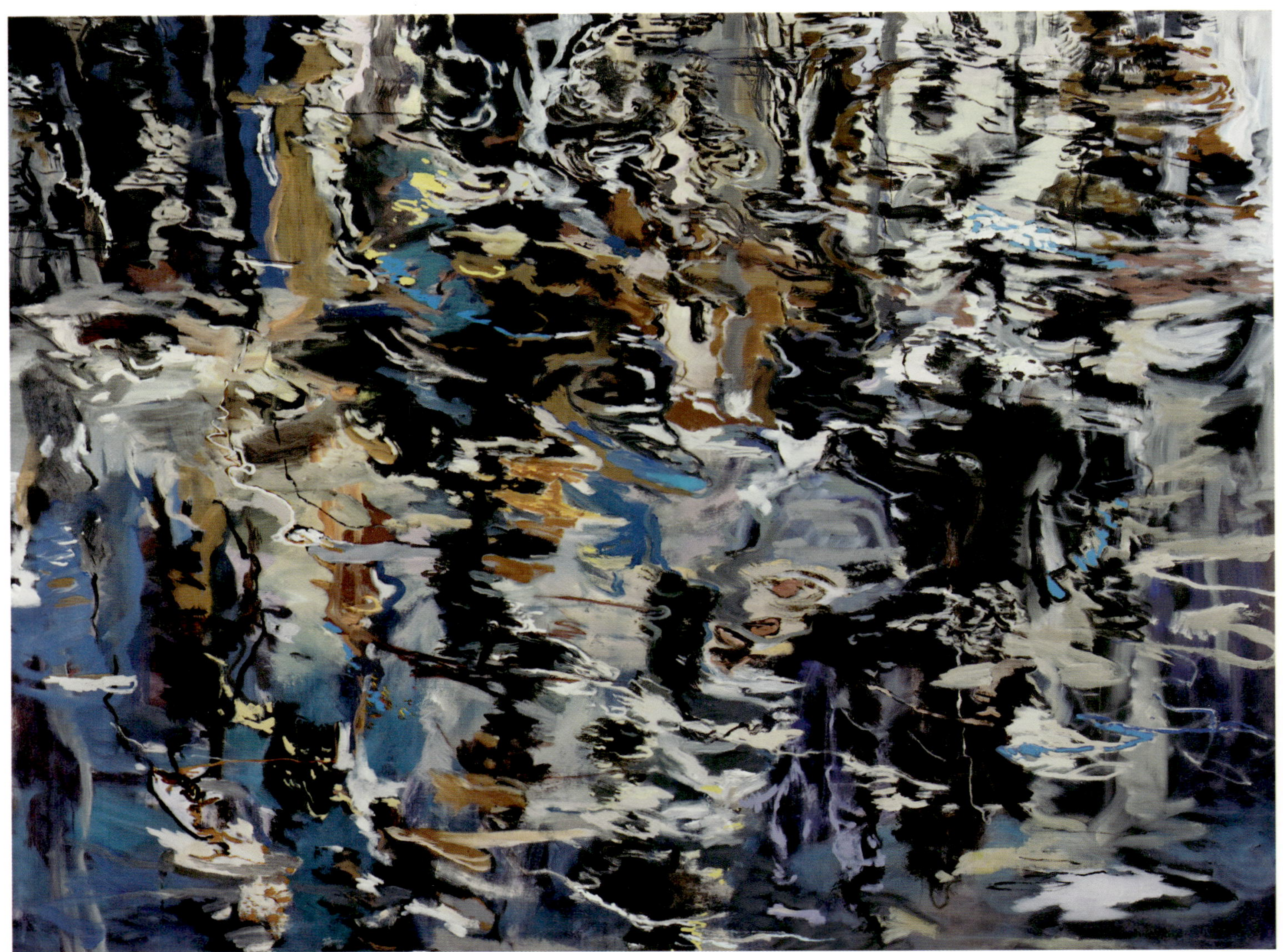

New Rockland Canal #3, Bobcaygeon, undated, [c. 2000], acrylic on canvas, 79 × 102 in.

DAVID ALEXANDER, AND BEING SURROUNDED BY THINGS WE HAVE NOT MADE

Ihor Holubizky

In spite of the heavy imprint of tumultuous social subject matter that weaves through art in the modern age, nature and the landscape – seemingly neutral and enchanting – remain fundamental to the artist's vision. The relationship summarized by Kenneth Clark sixty years ago still resonates: "[landscape painting] depends so much on the unconscious response of the whole being to the world which surrounds [the artist]."[1] Unlike the portrait – a relationship and communion – there is no corporeal transfer, no physiognomy to read or a psychoanalytical "window to the soul." Nature cannot protest "I don't look like that," nor express satisfaction for our job well done. Yet, as Clark noted, much can be poured into it. The long journey of the imagination reflects our ever-changing cultural and social awareness of our world, and of how we are part of nature.

A dramatic shift took place when the notion of *plein air* appeared – to paint directly from nature as evidence of "truth to the view" and a faith in nature. The foundational terrain is occupied by five giants of landscape painting from the late eighteenth to the early twentieth century: John Constable, J.W.M. Turner, Gustave Courbet, Paul Cézanne, and Claude Monet. The outcome was Impressionism, which captured the imagination of the public and retains the attention of art history. The term has migrated into every modern national school, including that of Canada, but also created a stranglehold on "minor" painters.[2] The Canadian landscape was in turn hijacked by the Group of Seven in the formative years of the twentieth century, whose art promoted an attitude and style that has come to stand for the aspirations for a new nation. I hesitate to bring up the Group of Seven in the context of David Alexander's work because it is too easy to presume a painting lineage, even if they draw on a similar topography. Likewise, it would be an error to conflate the promotion of the Group's Mystic North with Alexander's wholly different enterprise.[3] Alexander's work brings to mind the "foot soldier" artist, and in a literal way.[4] Rather than style, though that is undeniably present in his work, it is the impulse to travel and to express the under-observed that informs Alexander's art as a matter of fact rather than a virtue, without presuming that direct painting is the sole measure of a true experience. For example, Alexander's "water observed" works freeze fleeting reflections, light, and colour, but in the end it is the palette of paint at hand and the choices made that constitute the reality.[5] The eye and mind are the agents for a thought-provoking experience, and not all impressions need be Impressionism. It is also interesting to note that in 1949 Clark regarded Impressionism as "a short and limited episode in the history of art, [that] has long ago ceased to bear any relation to the creative spirit of the time."[6]

A more compelling and useful trajectory to apprehend and appreciate Alexander's undertaking is through Bernard Smith's 1978 essay *Art as Information*. In this essay, Smith returns to his seminal research on the artists of the three voyages of Captain James Cook in the second half of the eighteenth century, first published in the book *European Vision and the South Pacific* (1960).[7] The Cook artists were the first Western artists to see and systematically record landscapes that were outside of the European experience. Beyond the need for documentary or illustrative drawing (which took the form of watercolour painting), the challenge of the moment was to "stress invention but minimize the illustrative and documentary components of perception."[8]

Artist-draughtsman Sydney Parkinson (Scottish, c. 1745–1771) was on the first voyage of 1768–71. In his journal, Parkinson described observations of water as the *Endeavour* rounded Cape Horn at the tip of South America and sailed into the Pacific. Smith commented: "the conventional wisdom of art history informs us that the French Impressionists were the first to see and to paint the colour in shadows. Yet here a century before is a young artist describing with precision the purples he sees in shadows and the effects of broken colour on water that reads like a recipe for an impressionist painting."[9] Parkinson didn't commit his observations to paint: he was too young, had only brief and circumscribed training, and died

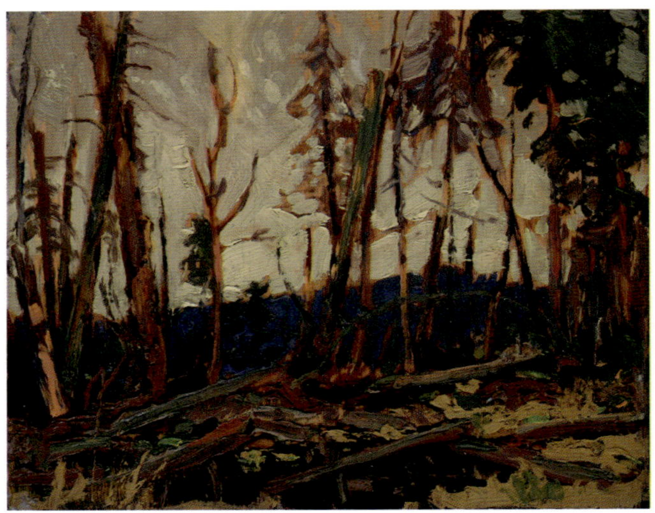

Tom Thomson, *Burnt Country, Evening*, 1914, oil on plywood, 8.5 × 10.5 in. Photo © NGC.

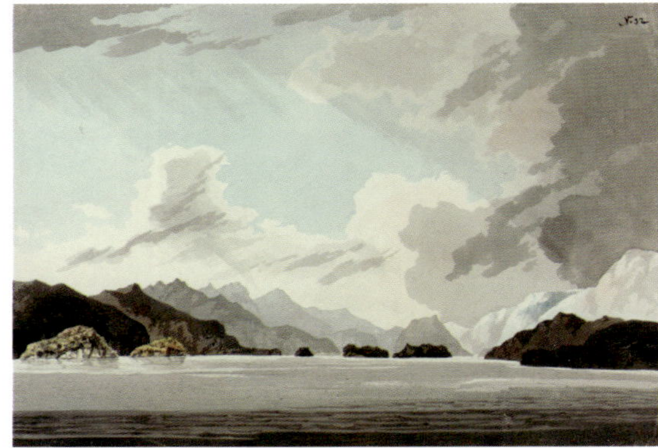

William Hodges, *View, possibly of Dusky Bay, New Zealand*, State Library of New South Wales, Sydney, Australia.

on the voyage. The breakthrough fell to William Hodges
(British, 1744–1797) during the second voyage of 1772–75.
Hodges was better equipped; he had studied with Welsh
landscape painter Richard Wilson (1714–1782), considered the
father of British landscape painting. In the Antarctic and then
in the tropics, Hodges was witness to new and unique plays
of light, and invented a visual language by intuitively adapting
watercolour training and techniques. One can wonder why,
but perhaps the answer is simply an inexplicable need to do
so: the influence of experiencing a previously unknown place.
Smith wrote:

In the Antarctic … Hodges preferred the use of wash
for capturing special effects of light [and] records not
only the water reflections in the cavernous interiors of
the icebergs but also the curious effect of the low northern sun upon the ships' sails; working with an economy
he achieves sharp optical effects. [In the tropics] Hodges
began to seek an optical rather than a plastic re-presen-
tation of reality by dispensing progressively with the use
of half-tone and sharpening his contrasts … Hodges
working under the pressure of a geographic imperative
[came] to paint what Constable [called] half a century
later, "a natural history of the skies."[10]

There was a legion of landscape foot soldiers in the twentieth century – and even radical modernists who were caught in
the "lure of the local"[11] – but I will turn instead to American
Rockwell Kent (1882–1971), whose work can divide art histori-
ans: there are those who are staunchly in the Kent camp and

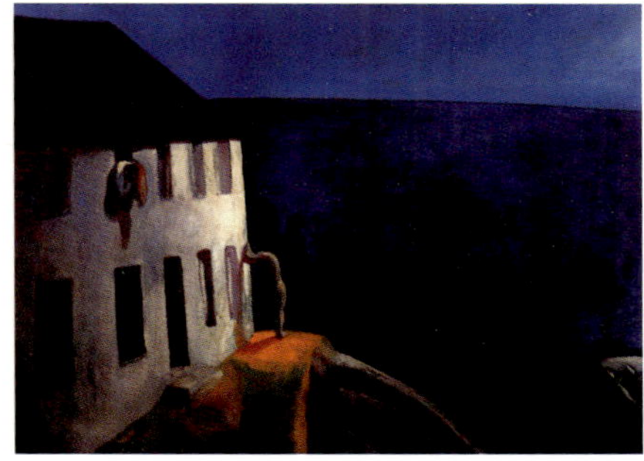

Rockwell Kent, *House of Dread,
Newfoundland*, 1915, oil on canvas,
27.75 × 37.75 in. Plattsburgh State
Art Museum, Plattsburgh, NY.

others who dismiss him as merely an illustrator of books. Kent
was something of a loner, an eccentric, as well as a political
radical. He travelled along less-trodden paths: Newfoundland,
1914–15; Alaska 1918–19; Tierra del Fuego, 1922–23; as well as
several trips to Greenland between 1929 and 1935. By this time
the camera could have done the work, but Kent was driven to
"live the view" and moved between the proposition of objective information and the intangibles of observation (what
comes through the eye, what is felt through the skin). In a
letter to New York art critic Dr Christian Brinton from Fox
Island, Alaska in the winter of 1919, Kent wrote: "I crave
snow-topped mountains, dreary wastes, and the cruel Northern Sea with its hard horizons at the edge of the world where
infinite space begins [but] this sojourn in the wilderness is
in no sense an artist's junket in search of picturesque material
for brush or pencil. … In living and recording these experiences, I have sensed a fresh unfolding of the mystery of life."[12]
The letter was in fact a journalist trick that Brinton encour-
aged. It accompanied his introduction to the exhibition of
Kent's Alaskan work in New York the same year. A passage

from Kent's Greenland journals, published as *Salamina* in 1935, continues and underscores the lure of locality for him: "Picture a temperate sea and mountain view; clear day, late afternoon in fall; blue sea and golden-purple shadowed land, and pale-blond lower sky; purple to gold, pale to deeper-toned. Now, into that, like a shaft of sunlight into a lamplit room … so clean, sharp, dazzling that it almost hurts."[13]

The dazzle experienced by Kent in solitude has its "in company" counterpoint, an anecdote about artists and the landscape related by art historian Heinrich Wölfflin. It is all the more noteworthy because Wölfflin uses it in his introduction to *Principles of Art History* (that is to say, a "principle of history" beginning with how artists respond):

> Ludwig Richter [1803–1884] relates … how once, when he was in Tivoli as a young man, he and three friends set out to paint part of the landscape, all four firmly resolved not to deviate from nature by a hair's-breadth; and although the subject was the same, and each quite creditably reproduced what his eyes had seen, the result was four totally different pictures … For the art historian, there is nothing surprising in this observation. It has long been realised that every painter paints "with his blood.[14]

To come full circle, Bernard Smith cites Wölfflin's assertion that "vision itself has a history" and proposes that a "precondition for the creation of that kind of vision, which seeks an aesthetic reality in a series of impressions, is the practice of art as an informational activity."[15] This reality is not an adherence to the factual – as if a slave to the view, a studio practice, or the comfort zone of a particular mannerism – but what plays out in the senses and "in the blood" to inform painting decisions.

Another leap ahead now, to passages from David Alexander's diaries. They are not offered as evidence of a conscious trajectory from the Cook Voyage artists to Rockwell Kent and

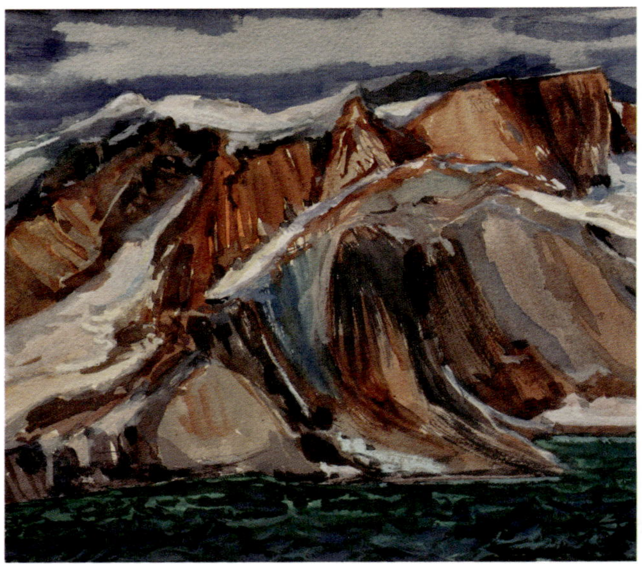

Remnants [Baffin Island], 1993, gouache, 8 x 9 in.

others, but are witness to the impulse and necessity to maintain a journal as it relates to the visual experience. From North Ellesmere Island, 23 July 1998, Alexander wrote: "I went for a short walk after dinner and found clam shell fossils, petrified wood and coral from when the Arctic was a tropical swamp … From my tent door I view an ice cap on the far side of the valley and glaciers tumbling into other valleys. From the lower valley looking upwards there are huge boulders fractured from the thermal shock of freezing and thawing. Small ponds of melt water lead up to where I have meat soaking in a pool of water." From his Greenland and Baffin Island sojourn in 1994, Alexander's diary describes an inventiveness, using materials at hand, from nature: "Did a drawing today using iron rock that I had crushed into powder with a knife. I mixed the powder with coffee, and used spit as a binder. For colour I used purple and red flower petals from the low bushes in the valley and to colour the water I used a small blueberry." Later, he writes an impressionistic entry on sound, which cannot be embodied in pictorial space, but is nonetheless significant to the experience: "[Icebergs] make the most incredible sounds as they break up and roll over. They grind, groan and creak, punctuated with very loud, haunting shrieks. Finally they break apart with the explosiveness of cannon fire." In an interview, Alexander spoke of the immediate and unexpected aspects – how he arrives to a moment and vision – and one incident at Emma Lake in Saskatchewan: "I am out in a row boat and a storm is coming … very fast, and there is lightning and thunder. It was so exciting and I was overwhelmed by it, and I kept on drawing. As it got closer, I realized that I am in an aluminum boat

in water and [there was] a chance of being fried. … As I get older [I] watch the conditions a little bit more, but I know that I belong within that landscape."[16]

To continue Alexander's "belonging" comment, an inescapable fact is that his landscapes are of some different order. And while his depopulated paintings might be taken for granted, they are not depopulated for the same reasons that Group of Seven works are. The Cook artists, on the other hand, depicted everything in keeping with the nature of their assignment: people, places, and things. Yet Alexander is aware of the social contact in remote places, the impact it has on him, and in turn, a conscious omission:

> I try to go places … where there is less population because I find it more interesting [and] do not put a human into the paintings … because the human is already there [and] already part of that landscape … The most important thing for me while I am in the landscape is to summarize or abbreviate the landscape into knowledge that I find applicable … You can[not] write about it and I have drawn that particular thing, but it is something that you are not in control of. Nature does not allow you to control it.[17]

This is, to repeat Clark's assertion, an "unconscious response of the whole being to the world."

Other evidence of this response can be seen in Alexander's bookworks. These are lesser known than his paintings for the simple and practical reason that books cannot be displayed

using the same conventions as paintings and works on paper,
yet they are of equal importance to his practice. There is
a one-to-one relationship; a book needs to be held in the
hand – the natural viewing distance – and the pages turned.
The drawings are not, as he has emphasized, sketches for
studio work, but are finished works unto themselves, and
like his diary journals, a travel companion. Alexander's
WORD/LAND book came about when he felt that images
and text had equal interest and, as he wrote, he "incorporated
them into a book of places and events while collecting information about the land."[18] That information makes up a
complex graphic language that expresses what is in front
of him, and what is happening elsewhere in the world. The
cover has a sympathetic resonance, a heavy card made from
Saskatchewan wheat stalks.

Alexander's work and commentary tell us that the age of
exploration and visual exploration has not come to an end.
And how could it? The landscape sits outside of historical
time; it is "forever there and eternal," and cannot be taken for
granted. By the same token, there is discovery and a consciousness in the act of making landscape art that remains apart from
other, more tumultuous, art of the contemporary age.

NOTES

1 Kenneth Clark, *Landscape into Art* (London: John Murray, 1949, third
edition 1952), 134.

2 Bernard Smith argues that while *plein air* painting was a revolutionary
development, "we cannot reduce the explanation of the emergence of impressionism as a style either in France or Australia to an account of *plein air*
sources." Bernard Smith, "An Australian Impressionism?" in *The Death of
the Artist as Hero* (Melbourne: Oxford University Press, 1988), 242. While
Smith proposes that Australian painters linked with impressionism did
not need to follow Monet's techniques – and only the "vaguest hints of a
programme" (245) – the problem of association remains as a habit of mind.
This distinction and localization is evidenced in modern age art in Asia,
ironic as some of the French Impressionists took their cues from Japanese
prints. As a return and volley, in the late Meiji period, the artist-teacher
Ishii Hakutei declared that Western art was the portal through which
every Japanese artist must pass. I am not conflating Japan for Asia alone –
the stories of modern art in China, Korea, and "elsewhere" have their
own trajectories.

3 *The Mystic North* was the title of Roald Nasgaard's 1984 Art Gallery of
Ontario exhibition and accompanying book. Nasgaard looked beyond the
national school origin-mythology to examine and explore – as described
in the subtitle – "Symbolist Landscape Painting in Northern Europe and
North America, 1890–1940."

4 While Constable et al. contributed to the paradigm shift of visual lan-
guages towards Impressionism, three were also staunchly regional landscape
painters: Constable in the Essex-Suffolk area of England; Courbet in
Ornans, and Cézanne in Provence. Monet travelled and painted widely, but
is most closely associated with his best-known "locality work" in Giverny.

5 Alexander takes note of responses to this work: "I am fascinated by how

people … all of a sudden [are] seeing water and reflections [as if looking at nature] for the first time." *David Alexander: Moving Targets: In Flux* (Vernon: Vernon Public Art Gallery, BC, 2010), 31.

6 Clark, *Landscape into Art*, 94. What Clark could not predict in 1949 was the museum promotion of Impressionism and its resilient public calling-card. In other words, what's-not-to-like.

7 Bernard Smith, *Art as Information, Reflections on the Art from Captain Cook's Voyages*. First presented at the annual lecture delivered to the Australian Academy of the Humanities, ninth Annual General Meeting, Canberra 16 May 1978, 84; later as a chapter in Smith's *Imagining the Pacific, In the Wake of the Cook Voyages* (New Haven: Yale University Press, 1992).

8 Ibid., 87.

9 Ibid., 92–3.

10 Ibid., 97–8.

11 One example is the Ukranian David Burliuk (1882–1967), who was deeply involved in the modern-radicalism of Der Blaue Reiter and Moscow-Russian Futurists, c. 1907–18. While in Japan from 1920–22, en route to the United States, and promoting his view of futurism to like-minded Japanese artists, he produced numerous impressionistic paintings and watercolours of the land, and wrote of this "communion" with a "new land." See Ihor Holubizky, "David Burliuk in Japan," in *Futurism and After: David Burliuk 1882-1967*, eds. Myroslav Shkandrij, Myroslava Mudrak, Ihor Holubizky (Winnipeg: Winnipeg Art Gallery, 2008), 27–31.

12 Rockwell Kent, *Wilderness: a journal of quiet adventure in Alaska* (1920, republished by Wesleyan University Press, 1996), xxxi and xxxiii.

13 Rockwell Kent, *Salamina* (Wesleyan University Press, 2003), 306.

14 Heinrich Wölfflin, *Principles of Art History* (New York: Dover Publications Inc., seventh edition, 1932), 1.

15 Smith, *Art as Infromation*, 102.

16 David Alexander, interview by Lubos Culen, 21 April 2010, in *David Alexander: Moving Targets: In Flux*, 17.

17 Ibid.

18 David Alexander, email message to author, 10 December 2010.

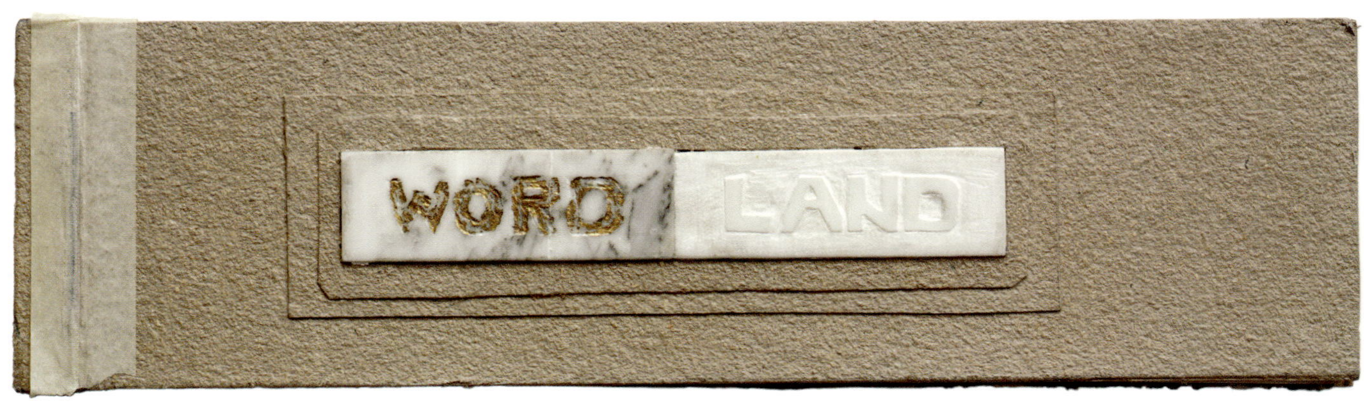

PLATE 19

WORD/LAND, 1998, artist's book, mixed media, 8 × 30 in.
Front outside cover

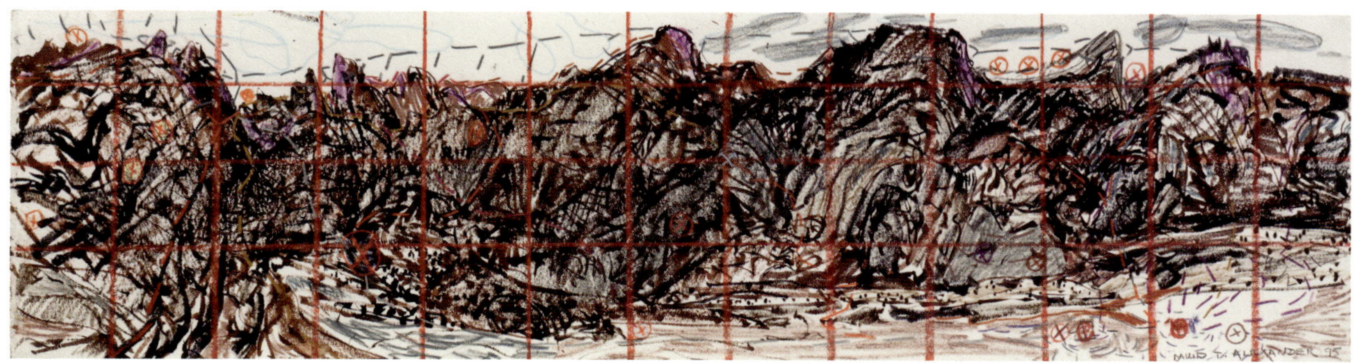

PLATE 19.1

Western Sites for Journalists

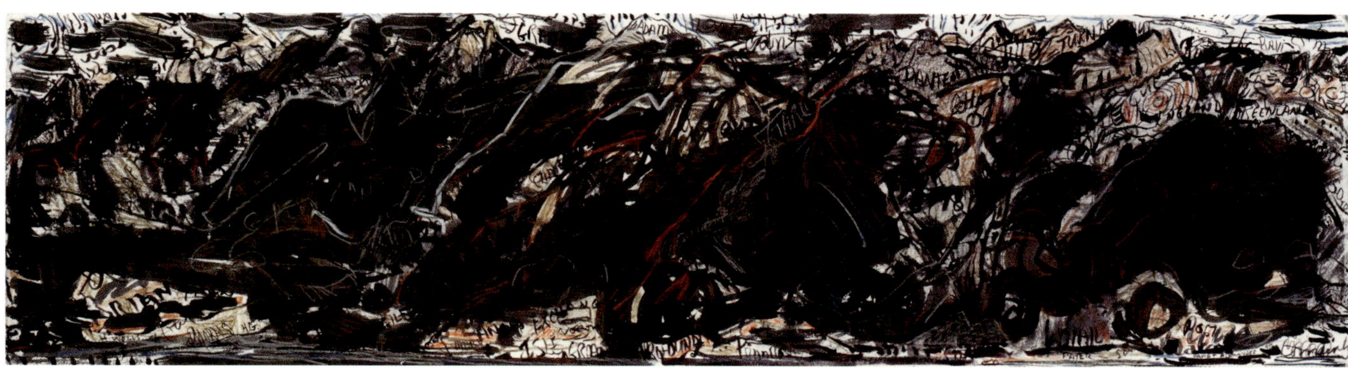

PLATE 19.2

Europeans' Greenland Renamed Landscapes of No Name Form

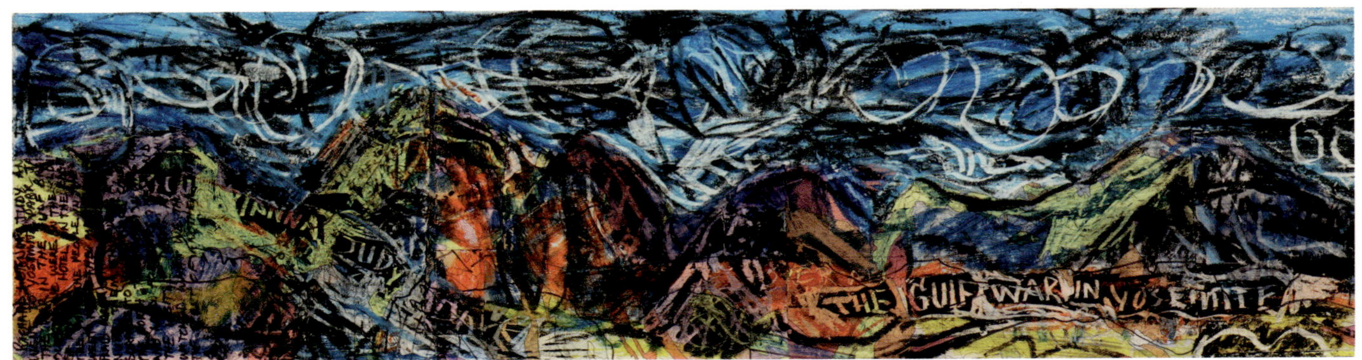

PLATE 19.3

The Gulf War in Yosemite Park

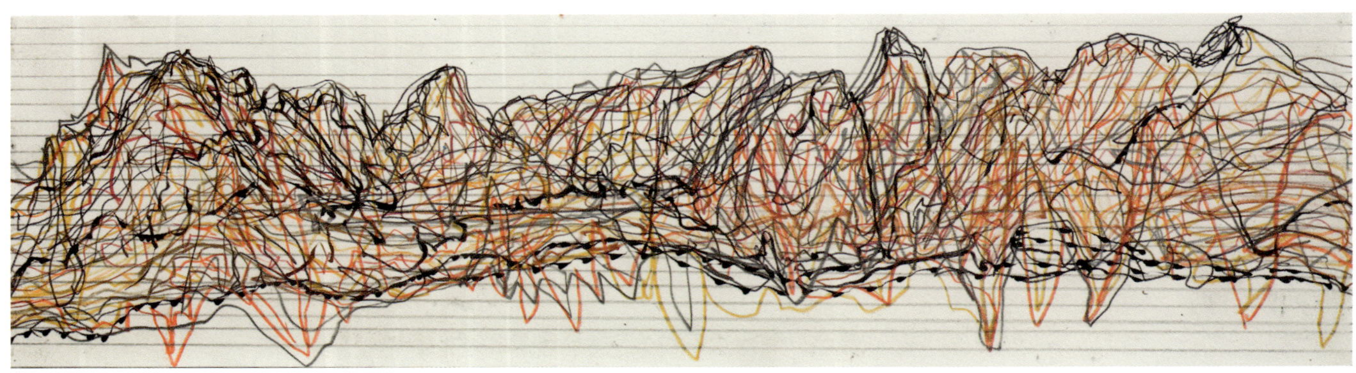

PLATE 19.4

T.S. Monk Jazz which is a probable earthquake cause of another line drawing of a continuous nature

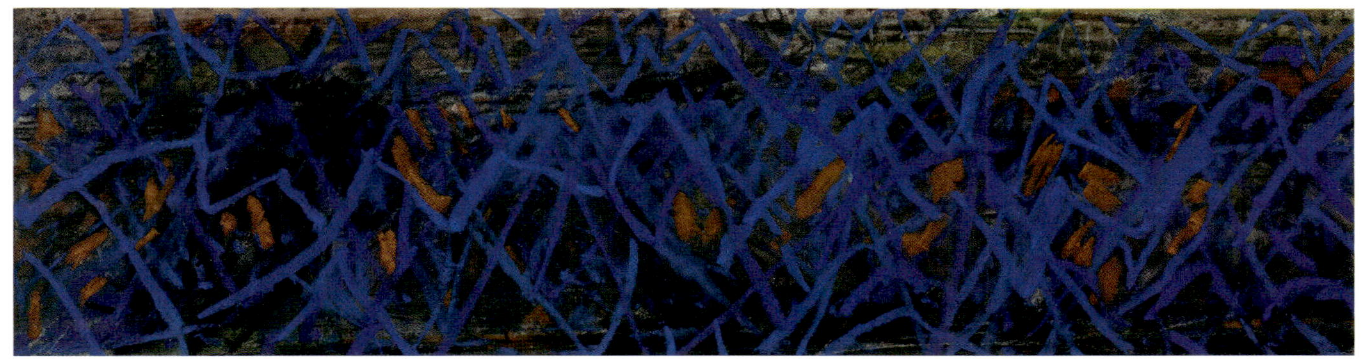

The Story of Two Letters: A Wall is a Mountain and a Mountain is a Wall

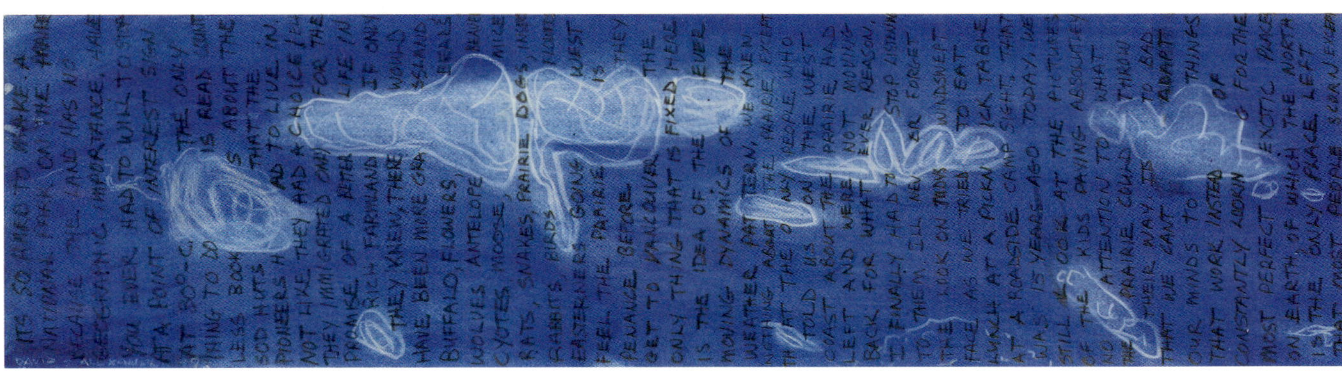

What a Prairie National Park Should Be

PLATE 19.7

A Dark Landscape through a Storm of Words

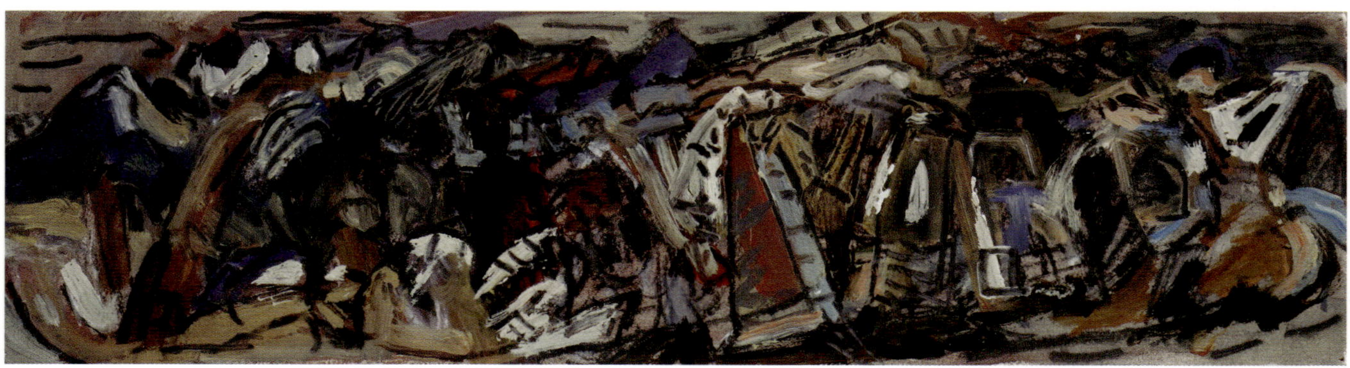

PLATE 19.8

Words Aside: a stone land

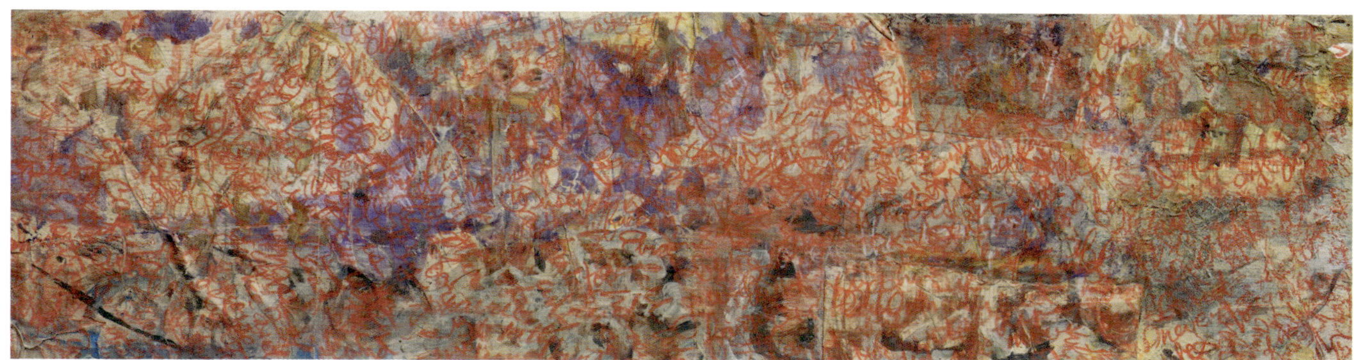

The abuse of words in the land

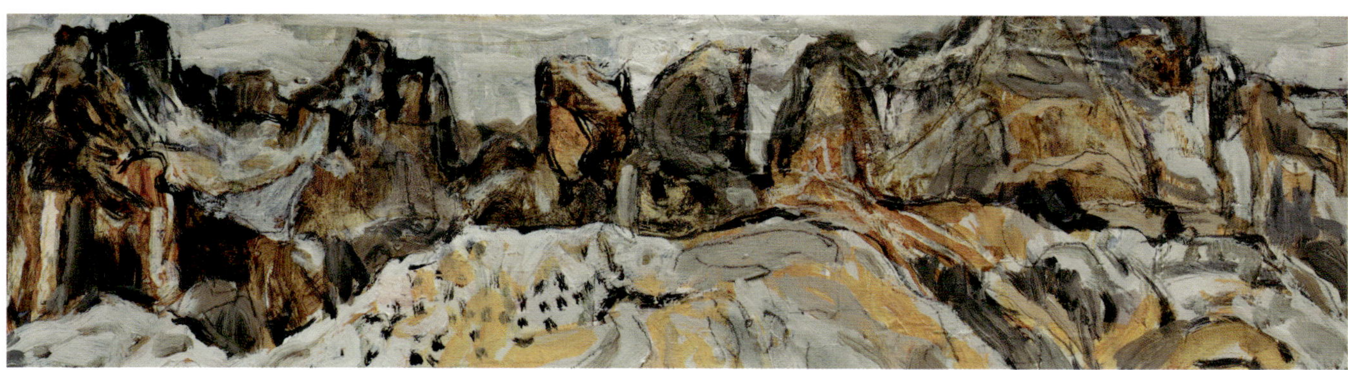

Does the word top?

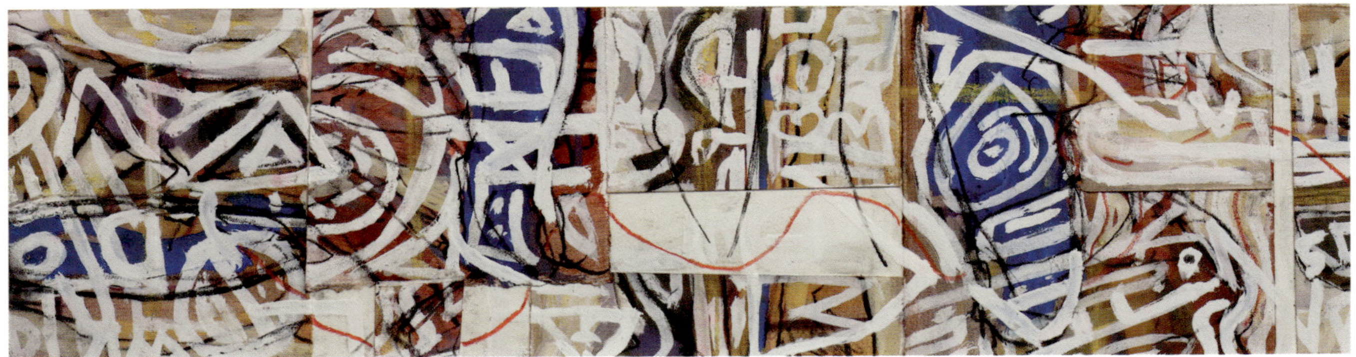

PLATE 19.11
Refigured Land and alphabet

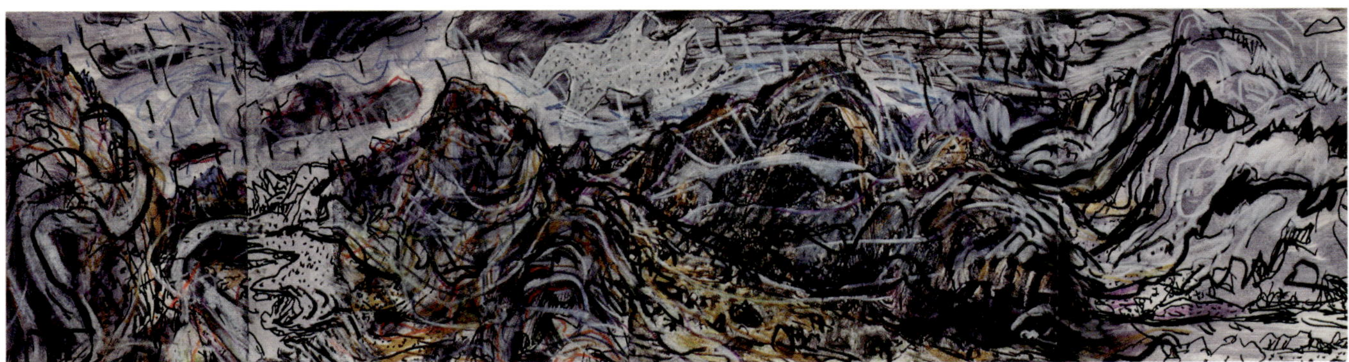

PLATE 19.12
Canada's Music

A LAND OF WATER

Gilbert Bouchard

Canada has long seen itself as a land filled with hewers of trees and drawers of water – a strong, self-reliant, resource-oriented nation, sure of itself in the woods, both real and metaphorical. Following logically from this vision is the physical reality of our nation being filled with trees for hewing and water for drawing, as well as a matching symbolic reality of a forested and lake-rich homeland of the mind. From this notion of active wilderness also follows the sense that Canadians of all stripes, from lumberjacks to politicians to artists, must somehow come to grips with this forested and lake-fronted reality in a fashion that is both practical and sublime. In short, much as atheists are not welcome in foxholes, wilderness greenhorns are denied full Canuck bragging rights. To challenge Pierre Berton, a true Canadian is not really the person skilled enough to make love in a canoe without tipping, but the person lake-and-forest-besotted enough to consider that skill one that would need to be put to use, never mind honed. The upshot of this centuries-long Canadian obsession is a nation in love with their shore-hugging cottages (or camps, cabins, or whatever regional variant you call the rough-hewn home that is between the trees and lapping waves), as well as a country of artists all taking their turns painting that famous iconic lonely tree, huddling beside the rough waters of Point Wherever-They-May-Be.

As a true Canadian landscape painter, David Alexander has not stinted on his duty to nation, nor to forest glade and wide open blue, embracing the broad mythic reality that this subject matter implies for the country. But Alexander tackles these canonic subjects in his own quixotic and naturally deconstructive fashion. Since the 1980s with his tree images, and his water portraits from the early years of this century, Alexander has been seeking to "take the myth apart" vis-à-vis the familiar call of waterfront and glade, starting with the notion that while this subject matter particularly enchants Canadians, it is a deeply universal trope. "It's an unquestionable given," says Alexander in a personal interview in front of an array of recent paintings of water and trees, "that this wooded, watered reality does affect us as Canadians. The real debate is how it affects us, especially those of us living on the tree-and-lake-sparse prairies, and how this affects our larger sense of identity."

"Is the image of a tree a surrogate for a human?" Alexander goes on, "Yes it is. We need to omit that as a question and put the tree into context with the history of the forest across human existence. Yes, we have swallowed the myth of the land

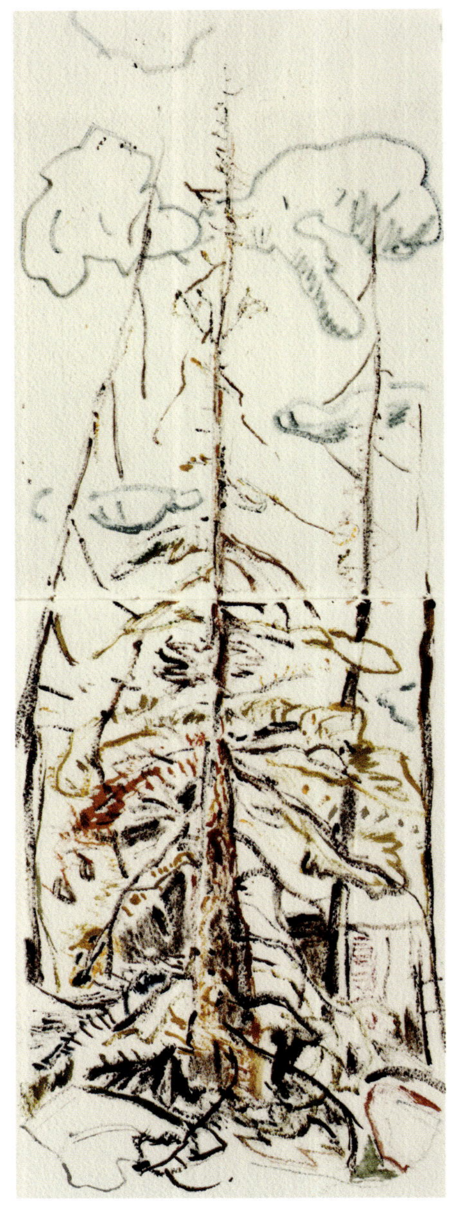

hook, line, and sinker, and we are also seeing a deconstruction of that myth. This only follows, that as we dismantle the myth, it comes back again in other forms."

When Alexander talks of history he is talking as much about his own multi-generational relationship with tree and shore as he is about a drier, intellectual approach fed by reading and academic debates. As the child of a tugboat captain on the BC coast, Alexander grew up dragging the nation's endless resources up and down the rocky edges of the western edge of the country. "I now find myself looking back at those landforms, the influence of that experience," he says. Going one step further, the artist equates his movement from direct resource manipulation to indirect representation with a similar paradigm shift endured by earlier generations who slipped seamlessly from the era of buggies and horse whips to automobiles. It is a lateral movement from the historic myth of resource to a more contemporary sense of nationhood. The upshot of this paradigm shift is a dual artistic reality for Alexander: first, he sees himself as being so colonized by the endless landscape – real and mythic – that he cannot paint without painting landscape. Second, he has had to earn the right to paint landscape, realizing that from the get go, the landscape in which he lives is not that defined by European and then Canadian painters. Typical of any artist working with a subject located at the fringes of artistic reality, as a newly minted prairie landscape painter in the 1980s,

Untitled [Cathedral Lakes Park, BC], 2006, watercolour, 17 × 6 in.

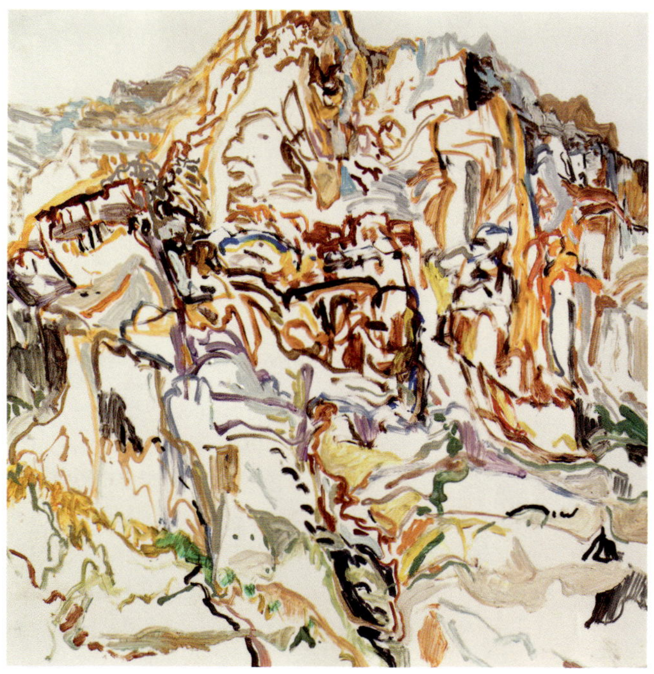

Rocky Scratch [Rockies], 2004, gouache and ink, 10.25 × 9.75 in.

Alexander found himself working through the history of the landscape trope. He was never afraid to tweak the expectations of what a vista should or should not be. The more daunting task was dragging the Canadian vista, in his words, "kicking and screaming into the twenty-first century." As a case in point, when asked about his tendency to not portray the tops of the mountains in his now iconic alpine vistas, Alexander replied that he does not *need* to paint them in. "The viewer naturally fills in the missing parts in these paintings," he explains, "we know that the mountain tops are there and what they look like," underlining that his paintings have always been participatory. Rather than providing the viewer with an objective and spread-out-in-front-of-you vista, Alexander gives the art lover a subjective view, more akin to that of the hiker when climbing a mountain and true to the reality of the land-scape as a place that is occupied. Alexander goes on to say that, ironically enough, he feels the mountain tops are not that pretty and are not missed in his paintings.

This same extreme subjectivity on his part is evident as well in the artist's tree-and-water paintings. If his tall moun-tains are devoid of their tops, Alexander's tree portraits are all about tops, as though painted from a viewpoint on the forest floor. Perhaps you are giving yourself a short respite during a forest hike, craning your neck to break the cacophonous monotony of tree trunks. In fact this point of view in his tree paintings was inspired by memories of his infant son lying in his crib, forced to stare upward. Alexander was spurred to imagine what this gaze would take in.

The situation is the same with the artist's water paintings. These are works that depict nothing but the reflective surfaces of bodies of water, the same view you get staring over the side of a canoe. Alexander has explored this in the past in his forestscape paintings. He is an avowed and accomplished outdoorsman and canoeist and paints from a deep, lived experience of the woods.

Talking with Alexander one quickly realizes the tension he feels as a person who both loves and lives the reality of the forest and lake. He chose to distance himself from a realistic approach to the subject, preferring one that is ripe for his own mining. He is a painter who skirts both realism and abstraction (it is notable that some viewers have mistaken his all-surface water reflection paintings to be abstract works). Instead, he embraces the notion that the land itself becomes abstract as soon as one is not directly connected or beholden to it. If Canada truly is a land of water, as Alexander says, then it is a land of quixotic impermanence, but also as solid as concrete. In a sense, Canada is only those places that exist in a photograph, a painting, or in one's memory. If one cannot step into the same river twice, to Alexander, this means being able to paint water surfaces that comprise everything, because of their inherent mutability: "I realized that these water surfaces hold all the landscape around them, including the sky. I see this in part because as a painter you are trained to see immensity, and there it was, in the water," he says. "Mind you, it is the small pond that has the greatest immensity of information in its reflective surface because it has to encompass so much due to its tight relationship with everything around it. The open ocean is where you finally return to water referring only to itself."

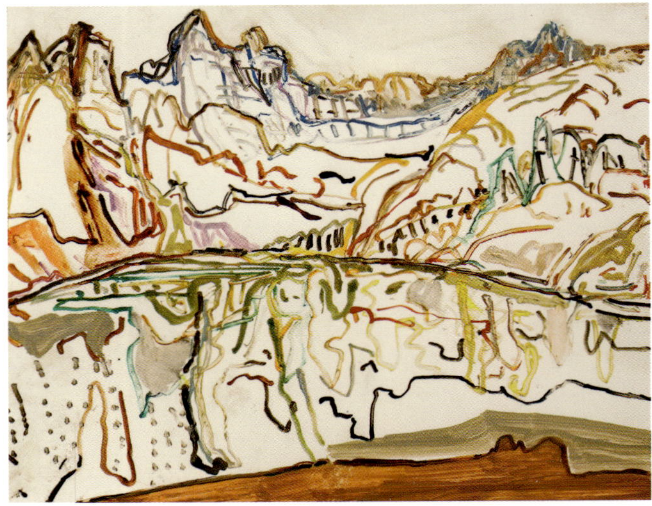

Agnes Lake [Rockies], 1998, gouache, 8 × 10 in.

More than an interplay of relationships, his richly coloured and heavily painted canvases also allow Alexander to both embrace and break free from artistic tropes. A viewer can focus on painting for painting's sake in Alexander's water vistas, identifying the brushstrokes that have been so energetically and skillfully applied. One can also compare the paintings to Alexander's source photographs and be struck at how realistic the paintings actually are. "These water paintings remind us all that our views of the landscape are always reflections – and they are fragmented and constricted," notes the artist. Following Alexander's logic, we can see his body of work as one that positions vista and landscape as equal partners.

Simon Schama wrote in his seminal book *Landscape and Memory* that "the wilderness, after all, does not locate itself, does not name itself … nor could the wilderness venerate itself."[1] In the same spirit, Alexander embraces the swirling eddies of self-referentiality in his work, feeling that the truth of painting is about painting, as well as about the idea: that "what" which the artist pursues. "To capture the viewer I have to realize that the first viewer is me, which means that I have to be very clear in making sure that I *see* what is most familiar with my relationship to the mountaintop, the tree, or the water's surface," he says. This is both a brave and broad personal mandate. Faced with rapid urbanization and the razing of natural resources (we have surely all read that the areas of clear-cut forest in British Columbia can be seen from outer space) our relationship to landscape may never have been so vital and critical – and so complicated. We are stuck awkwardly among myths: happy as hewers of trees and draw-ers of water, as well as feeling completely alienated from those activities. We may be deep in the woods, yet strangers to the true wilds. A contemporary landscape artist like David Alexander can show us to paths that twist toward dreams of green we do not yet know.

NOTE

1 Simon Schama, *Landscape and Memory* (New York: Alfred A. Knopf, 1995), 7.

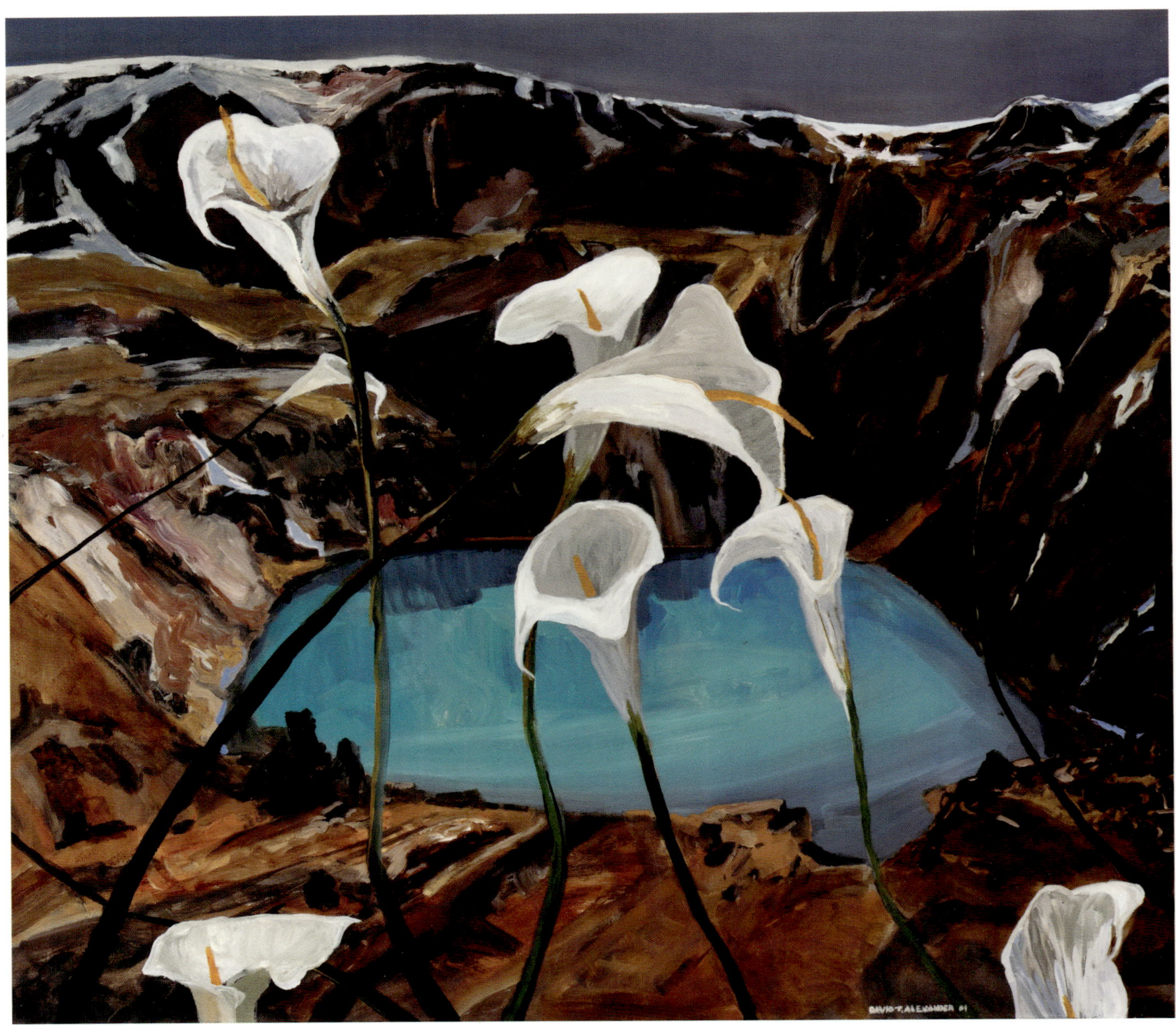

PLATE 20

Rims around the Entrance, 2001, acrylic on canvas, 60 × 68 in.

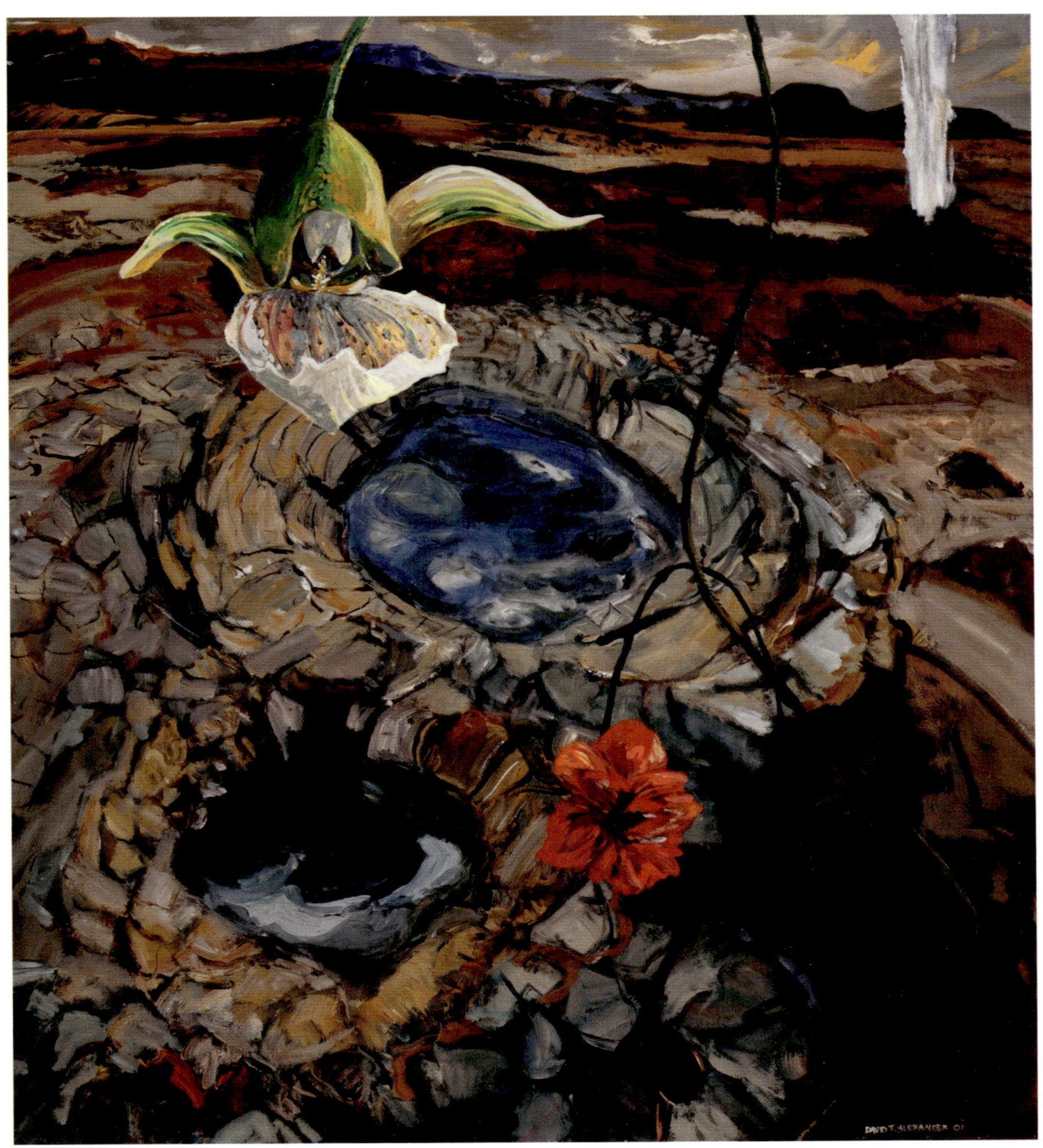

PLATE 21

Iceland's Earth's Kitchen, 2001, acrylic on canvas, 58 × 52 in.

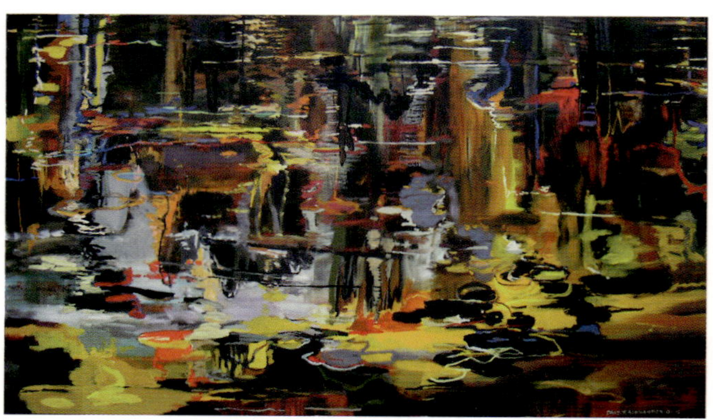

Morning under La Cloche, 2001–2, acrylic on canvas, 61 × 102.5 in.

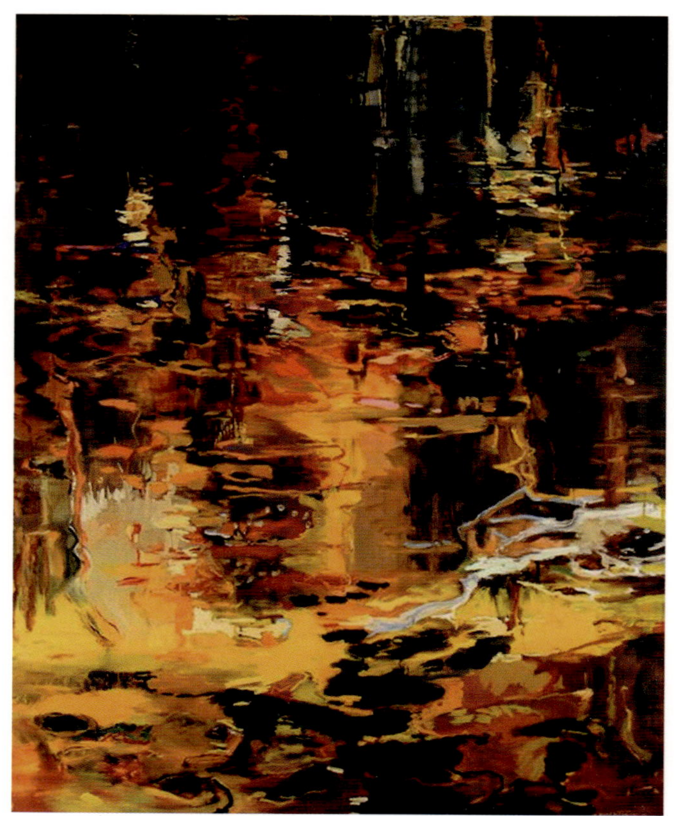

The Perfect Pond, 2002, acrylic on canvas, 83 × 65.5 in.

AN "OTHER" ICELAND:
MUSINGS ON THE ALEXANDER LANDSCAPE

Aðalsteinn Ingólfsson

Landscape painting is the single constant strain in the art of those two northern countries, Canada and Iceland. Though intermittently interrupted by the modernist quest for an urban aesthetic, it has proven remarkably resilient. In his 1949 study, Kenneth Clark lamented that nature "seemed too large and too small for imagination," that we had "lost faith in the stability of what we used hopefully to call 'the natural order,' and, what is worse, we know that we have ourselves acquired the means of bringing that order to an end."[1] Sixty years later, landscapes are still the lodestones of Canadian and Icelandic artists in their mediations of experience and imagination. Landscape art of one type or another, from fairly traditional painting to the installations and environmental pieces of Ólafur Elíasson, to name one Icelandic example, has shown itself able to absorb internationalist and modernist currents while remaining faithful to the specificities of place and history.

Tempting though it is to discuss the uncultivated expanses of Western Canada or Ellesmere Island and the Icelandic highlands in terms of a generic "Northern landscape" and "Northern mood" – after all, much of Canada extends considerably further north than does Iceland – there are too many other factors at work to make the comparison a perfect one. Though both countries can be said to be located at the geographical margins, their geologies and climates are different, not to mention the human factors: history, population patterns, and culture. All of which affect the way Canadian and Icelandic artists see and interpret their natural environment. In his great book, *Landscape and Memory*, Simon Schama contends that "all landscapes are culture before they are nature."[2] He means that landscapes are the elaborate constructs of the imagination of those who first colonize them, with the result that these constructs or visions gradually take the place of "nature as itself" and become more real than their points of reference. What the landscapes of Canada and Iceland have in common is that both of them, at different times, have undergone a process of what we might call "mediation by culture" or "aestheticizing," before they were "set free" by later generations of artists who realized that what they saw in the landscape did not correspond to the artistic conventions by which they were expected to abide. From the late eighteenth century onwards, painters from Britain chose to see the landscape of Canada in terms of the European pastoral tradition or incorporated it seamlessly into their imported visions of the sublime. It took the intimate and interpretative approach of the Group of Seven and Emily Carr, inspired by Northern European expressionism, to redress the balance in favour of nature "as itself." And as art history would have it, their interpretations have been repeatedly challenged by later generations of landscape painters.

Iceland is home to handicraft traditions dating back to the twelfth century in woodcarving, metalwork, and textiles. But there was no painting to speak of until the late nineteenth century, when Icelanders began to shake off nearly two centuries of poverty, bad climate, volcanic eruptions, and Danish misrule. Even then, Icelanders were without art schools and museums and thus depended on the Copenhagen Art Academy for their art education. Quite naturally, the paintings by Icelandic pioneers such as Þórarinn B. Þorláksson and Ásgrímur Jónsson show a strong influence from the largely literary nineteenth-century Romantic landscape tradition. Until the late 1920s these paintings were characterized by an idealization of nature that had its roots in Iceland's nationalist-romantic campaign for independence, not least because by then the country's landscape had become the emblem of its uniqueness. In effect, these early painters had to transform, to aestheticize, what one art historian has called a "harsh land of whimsical natural forces,"[3] and turn it into visions of eternal European summer. It took the conflagration of World War I and the harsh realities of the Great Depression to dispel this vision and turn artists such as Jóhannes Kjarval, Jón Stefánsson, and Finnur Jónsson towards a more realistic approach to the "real" landscape of the Icelandic interior: harsh, fantastic, and downright dangerous.

This is where the story becomes personal. As an Icelandic art historian and critic, I had written numerous books and articles on local landscape-based art, from the idealist painters of the early twentieth century to the mixed-media artists of the 1990s. By the end of the millenium it seemed to me that the aestheticizing attitude to landscape, which had characterized the efforts of our earliest painters, was making a comeback in Icelandic art. Perhaps it was inevitable, given the dominance of arid conceptual art during the 1970s, and the aggressive anti-aesthetic bias of the neo-expressionism that followed it. But it was an attitude I disliked, one that I railed against in my 1994 book on a Norwegian artist, Patrick Huse.[4] To paraphrase myself, I stated that the aestheticized landscape – what Simon Schama would call "landscape as myth" – had long ceased to enlighten, engage, or nourish us. It was like a song "grown old not from time but from wear … a song frayed and worn out," to quote American novelist William Kennedy in *Ironweed*. Apart from its highly suspect claims to "truthfulness," this kind of landscape contains too many unresolved problems, too much unfinished business. For one thing, there was – and is – the constant tug-of-war between the prosaic attitude of description and the poetic attitude of interpretation. Also, the whole notion of the "meaning" of a natural phenomenon, be it a tuft of grass or a mountain, was always too vague to engage the viewer except on a superficial level. But what bothered me most about this kind of landscape art was that it seemed unable to cope with the precariousness that characterizes our present relationship with nature. Just over a century ago, Cézanne claimed that only by immersing ourselves in nature could we gain a greater understanding of it. In fact, our ever-increasing understanding of nature only seems to have strenghtened our proprietary attitude to it. We have undermined it from the outside, as witnessed in the industrialized zones of Europe, Asia, and the Americas, and also from the inside, as scientists tinker with genes.

In my book on Huse I called for a new approach to landscape painting, one that would take in all the contradictions that we confront when facing nature. I imagined this painting as having a language of its own, what the great Italian writer Césare Pavese called an "instrument of complete expression." To him, such a language stands for a "space full of doubt, possessing its own range of meanings" which can't be conveyed in any other way. Through this language, the artist would express, with the utmost economy of means, "a general and comprehensive fact, a core of reality quickening and feeding,"[5] a whole organic growth of passion and human existence.

Implicitly, and perhaps most importantly, this would be a patently "constructed" landscape, free of all preconceived notions about what such a construct should look like. At the same time it would have enough in common with the natural landscape "as itself" to make us want to relate to it, to fathom its geography, and to find our place within it. To quote the American environmental writer Barry Lopez, "It should make us want to discover a way of dispelling our sense of estrangement, now a fact of life in the western world."[6] It seemed to me that Patrick Huse was one of very few painters I knew who believed in the constructed landscape as "an instrument of complete expression" capable of engaging our deepest emotions. But his paintings are certainly not com-

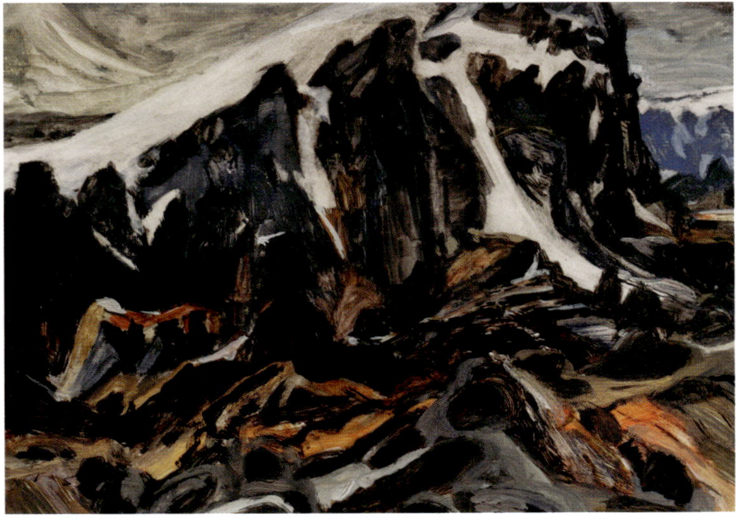

Baffin Walk [Baffin Island], 1997, gouache and ink, 8 × 11 in.

fortable to look at. They depict landscapes as heaps of organic matter disembowelled, turned inside out, and petrified, and suggest a world emptied of all life and all meaning.

In 1997 I travelled around Canada, lecturing on Icelandic art to the descendants of the early Icelandic settlers. Was I perhaps unconsciously looking for a another landscape painter, though perhaps not with Huse's apocalyptical zeal, feisty enough to take on the whole idea of landscape "as itself" and turn it on its head? At any rate, landscape as idea and reality was much on my mind as I made my way by plane over prairie, tundra, and the Rockies. Coming from a mountainous country myself, I wondered how Canadian landscape painters coped with the relentless flatness of the prairie. In Winnipeg I had an appointment with Meeka Walsh, editor of *Border Crossings*, a magazine that I had long admired. In the course of our conversation she handed me the latest issue of *Border Crossings* and in it was an in-depth interview by Robert Enright with Saskatoon-based painter David Alexander, whom I hadn't heard of before. I read it that night and was struck by the way in which Enright spoke about the "unease" that Alexander's paintings arouse in the viewer. That was certainly one of my reactions to the illustrations of his work published with the interview. And, to be frank, another was dislike: as a European, albeit a marginal one, I could tell where Alexander's roots were showing. There was something of Munch's "vast, infinite cry of nature" in his in-your-face vistas, and some of Hodler's bold, luminous colours, and coloured shadows. Perhaps most surprisingly – I didn't think anyone looked at them today – I even saw something of the turbulence of Kokoschka's Scottish landscapes. But this European underpinning, if that is the right word for it, was overlaid with brushstrokes of such visceral and relentless energy that every painting seemed on the verge of dissolution. It was the way Alexander put all his emotions on the line that unnerved me the most, especially his insistence on "feeling" his way into every bit of landscape that he chose to paint, taking it all apart and putting it back together until it looked both familiar and out of this world. He seemed, quite literally, to be pulling the rug from under the feet of the "nature lover," mocking one's presumed right of access to every part of God's creation. What finally won me over was Alexander's way with the prairie.

Instead of seeing it as a non-landscape, because of its lack of verticals, mountains, big trees, and other distinguishing features (rather in the way we Icelanders denigrate the flat landscape of Denmark), he seemed to regard it almost as the "mother of all landscapes." As he explained to Robert Enright: "In the prairie you can generally stand in one spot and take it all in. It comes to you, but in the mountains you have to go to it."[7] And what comes to Alexander in the prairie is the vast architecture of the heavens, what the artist calls "the craziness that's up in the sky." Not only does he paint what he sees in the skies, the thousand dramas that herald violent changes in the weather, but also what he would like to see happen up there. This gives his prairie sky paintings a visionary quality that one associates with artists like El Greco, who worked in sixteenth-and seventeenth-century Spain, or the Dutch Hercules Seghers, active in the same time period. Moreover, Alexander frequently takes liberties with the horizon itself, tipping it this way or that, or he changes its shape from convex to oval in order to construct a bird's-eye vision of the firmament. Or he compresses the prairie and sky into narrow vertical structures, forcing us to question our habitual horizontal reading of wide open spaces.

Once I got into Alexander's approach to landscape, what appealed to me most was his respect for it as "the other," an entity quite separate from our puny selves: mysterious, supremely indifferent to us, and quite deadly when crossed. This comes out in what Alexander calls his "enclosures," a fitting name for his paintings of forests. In them there is no concession to the pastoral or picturesque; the trees with their spiky branches are there to enclose, entangle, and eventually swallow up anyone venturing into their midst. The mountain paintings, especially the vertical ones, also present us with one dangerous view after another, rock faces prone to unleashing deadly avalanches of ice and boulders at any moment. I began to wonder what Alexander would be able to do with the landscape of my native Iceland, where you find the most spectacular cloud formations, as well as some of of the most unforgiving "natural attractions" on the European side of the Atlantic. On my return, I wrote him a letter asking him whether he would like to come to Iceland.

David Alexander visited Iceland twice, both times as a guest of the Hafnarfjörður Arts Centre, an institution with which I was then affiliated. His first trip was in the autumn of 1999; the second was three years later. Hafnarfjörður is a town of some 20,000 people located in the middle of a lava field, a fifteen-minute drive from Reykjavik. Another spot that is further out, situated on a barren coast, with a view of interminable lava fields as well as of Iceland's only aluminium smelter, is the former farmhouse of Straumur. This house been converted into a artists' workshop, with a couple of studio apartments for visiting artists from abroad. This is where David Alexander stayed during his time at the Hafnarfjörður Arts Centre. The manager of the Straumur house was an exuberant and highly eccentric sculptor named Sverrir Ólafsson who did well by Alexander, taking him on a number of hair-raising day trips into the countryside in his supercharged SUV. I met Alexander as soon as he had settled in. I found him to be exhilarating company, warm and en-gaging, full of opinions, knowledgable about the history of art, and inquisitive about everything that he saw: the age and

precise formation of the lava all around us, the type of boats that Icelanders of old used to fish from off the nearby coast (I didn't yet know about his early life on tugboats), the moss and lichen coating the pseudocraters and hollows in the lava, and the colours of the sheep that were grazing wherever there was a patch of green. Odd things seemed to delight Alexander, not in the least names: he was intrigued as to why a farm would be called Straumur, that is "sea current." Our bit of coast was also called "Vatnsleysuströnd," that is, "coast-without-natural-water." This pleased Alexander to no end, because it reminded him of Indian place names in Canada. Out of that arose much good-humoured and quite absurd banter about the early Indian tribes of Iceland.

During that 1999 visit to Iceland, Alexander was mostly without transport. He spent a lot of time hiking in the vicinity of Straumur, following old tracks in the lava made by farmers, fishermen, and sheep. The lava landscape and the violent forces that had created it were a source of endless fascination to him. That it was a relatively "young" landscape – this particular stretch of lava dates back some 12,000 years – clearly appealed to him, both emotionally and intellectually. Coming from a country with a bedrock that dates back billions of years, Alexander imagined himself standing on what he called "earth's egg-shell crust," as close to the forces of creation as he was going to get. He talked about feeling "giddy" in some of the lava-encrusted trenches that he came across, looking down into narrow rifts so deep that they have never been fathomed. Then there were the unexpected sound effects, from the steam vents, for example: burbling and hissing everywhere. Alexander was also suprised and impressed by Icelanders' equanimity in the face of possible volcanic eruptions or other natural disasters. After visiting painter Gunnar Örn on his farm close to Iceland's most famous (and quite active) volcano, Hekla, he mused: "People don't seem to fear the inevitable; they live with it quite comfortably and even joke about it." Alexander also liked to think that this potentially violent landscape would be able to withstand the encroachment of "culture" to a greater extent than most of the other places that he had visited.

Much like philosopher Arthur C. Danto on his visit to Iceland, Alexander was "fascinated by what looked like low abstract sculptures punctuating (the lava) surface. If naïve minds could have read the skies as a stage for deities, these protrusions might just be visible evidence of hidden artisan gnomes."[8] Strange, anthropomorphic imagery quickly found its way into Alexander's drawings and coloured sketches. In them we find constant interaction between the human form and natural elements, something which I hadn't seen in the work that he'd done in Canada. Drawings of dark, fantastic coagulations were worked and reworked until they started to sprout eyes, eyebrows, and noses, or conversely grotesque figures coalesced into jagged lava spires. At one point Alexander began to collect lava rocks that looked like small "troll" heads, with the intention of placing them in a neat row in front of a painted landscape. A day trip to Kleifarvatn, a desolate place in the vicinity of Straumur, and the site of heavily weathered tufa formations, yellow-rimmed hot springs, and emerald-coloured lakes, yielded Alexander's only pure "supernatural" painting, what looks like a view of a ghost tumbling into a crater. The geological formations at Kleifarvatn have also worked their wonders on other visiting artists, among them Norwegian painter Odd Nerdrum, who has repeatedly used them as backdrop to his mythological narratives.

Looking at the drawings and coloured sketches that Alexander did during that fruitful month at Straumur as a whole, as well as the finished Iceland-based paintings that he brought to his Hafnarborg exhibition of 2002, I now realize that not only was he pitting himself against a landscape unlike any other that he had encountered, but he was using this landscape to probe into Icelanders' relationship with nature. The ambivalence that characterizes the Icelanders' attitude to the so-called "hidden beings" within nature is brought out in the fine balance between the "natural" and the "supernatural" in Alexander's drawings of geological oddities. Then there is his tendency to draw peoples' faces in terms of weathered boulders, complete with surface cracks and ungainly pro-tuberances, as if they were extensions of nature. The works of humans: old dwellings, rusted fuel tanks, disintegrating row boats, and even a country graveyard with one fresh grave fenced off by rope, all of these are seen not as additions to nature, welcome or unwelcome, but as integral to it. In one funny drawing Alexander portrayed the people sitting in the milky waters of the Blue Lagoon – now one of Iceland's biggest tourist attractions – as denizens of the deep, with only their disembodied heads and shoulders emerging from what the artist called a "High-Tech Primordial Swamp."

I am left with an image from Alexander's 2002 exhibition in the Hafnarborg Cultural Centre. He had hung some large canvases with Icelandic motifs in a row on the central wall of

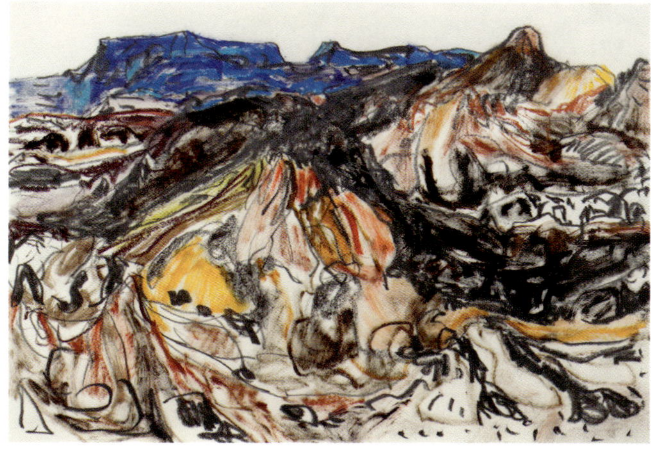

Black Time Flows Evidence [Iceland], 1999,
graphite and watercolour, 8 × 11.25 in.

the gallery. What distinguished these paintings from others in
the show were the flowers that Alexander had painted in the
foreground of some sombre and desolate landscapes, huge
luxurious red poppies swaying in the front of jagged lava cliffs,
an orchid bursting with fecundity on top of bubbling hot
springs, and a bunch of lilies engaging in a graceful dance
on the edge of a northern crater called *Víti* (Hell's cauldron).
To me these paintings seemed to encompass Alexander's
philosophy about landscape in general, and about the
Icelandic landscape in particular. In general terms, they
question our attemps to cultivate every bit of uncultivated
nature that we visit, physically or through art. But also,
through the very discordant juxtapositions of the hothouse
flowers and the unhabitable landscapes behind them,
Alexander seemed to hint at the absolute "otherness" of
the Icelandic landscape. For someone such as myself, who
thinks that civilization's influence on the natural world is
overrated, this is a heartening conclusion.

NOTES

1 Kenneth Clark, *Landscape into Art* (London: John Murray, 1949), 239.

2 Simon Schama, *Landscape and Memory* (New York: Alfred A. Knopf,
1995), 61.

3 Auður Ólafsdóttir, "Hið upphafna norður" (The northern sublime),
Morgunblaðið, 13 October 2001.

4 Aðalsteinn Ingólfsson et al., *Patrick Huse* (Oslo: Cappelen Forlag, 1994).

5 Césare Pavese, *Dialogues with Leucó* (Boston: Eridanos Press, 1989).

6 Barry Lopez, *Arctic Dreams* (New York: Vintage Books, 1986), xxiii.

7 Robert Enright, "The Pride of Influence: A Conversation with David
Alexander," *Border Crossings* 4, no. 3 (Summer 1997): 56.

8 Arthur Danto quoted in Kristín Guðnadóttir et al., *Kjarval* (Reykjavik:
Nesútgáfan, 2005), 537.

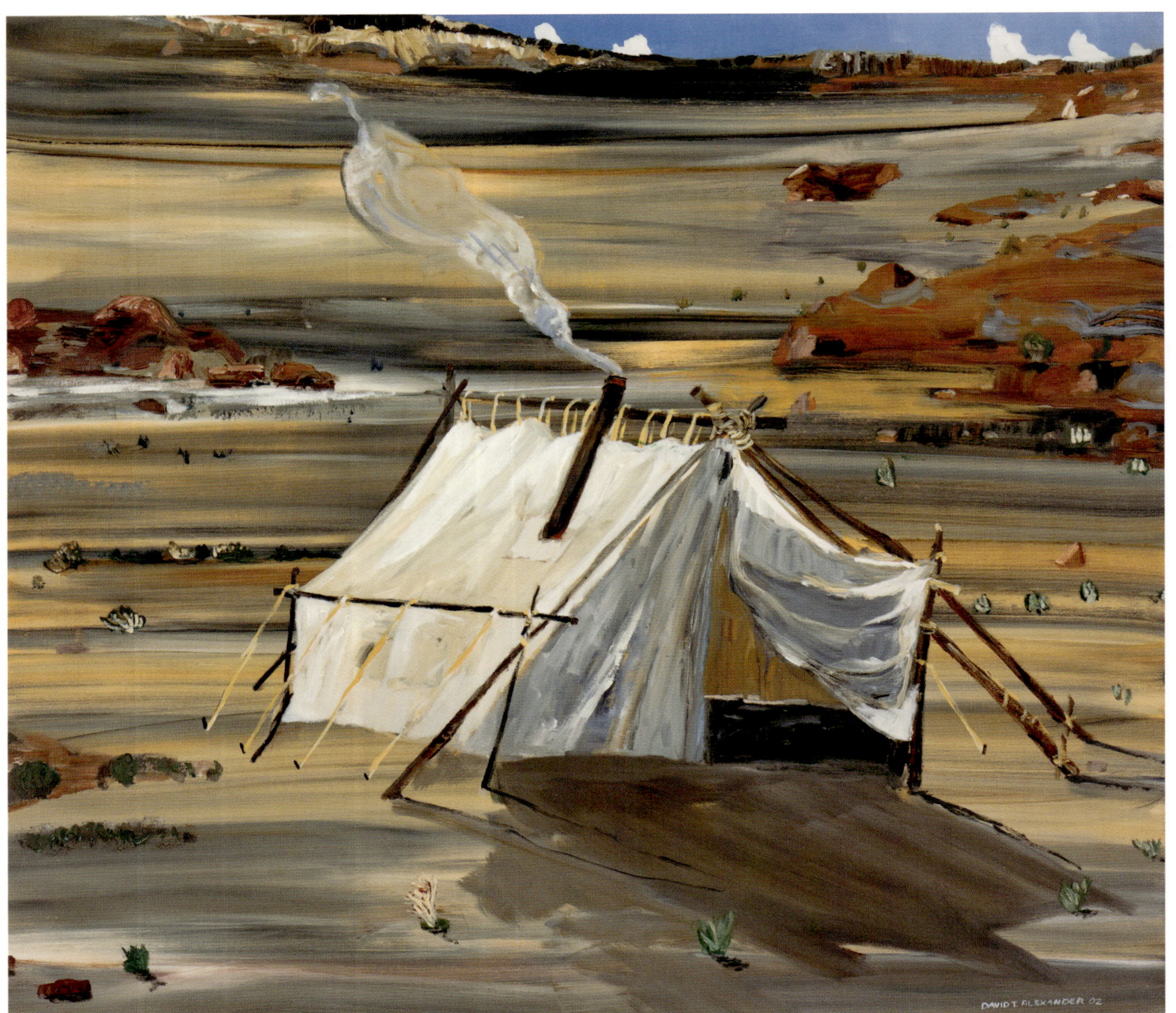

PLATE 24

You Go Knock on the Door, 2002, acrylic on canvas, 51.5 × 57.75 in.

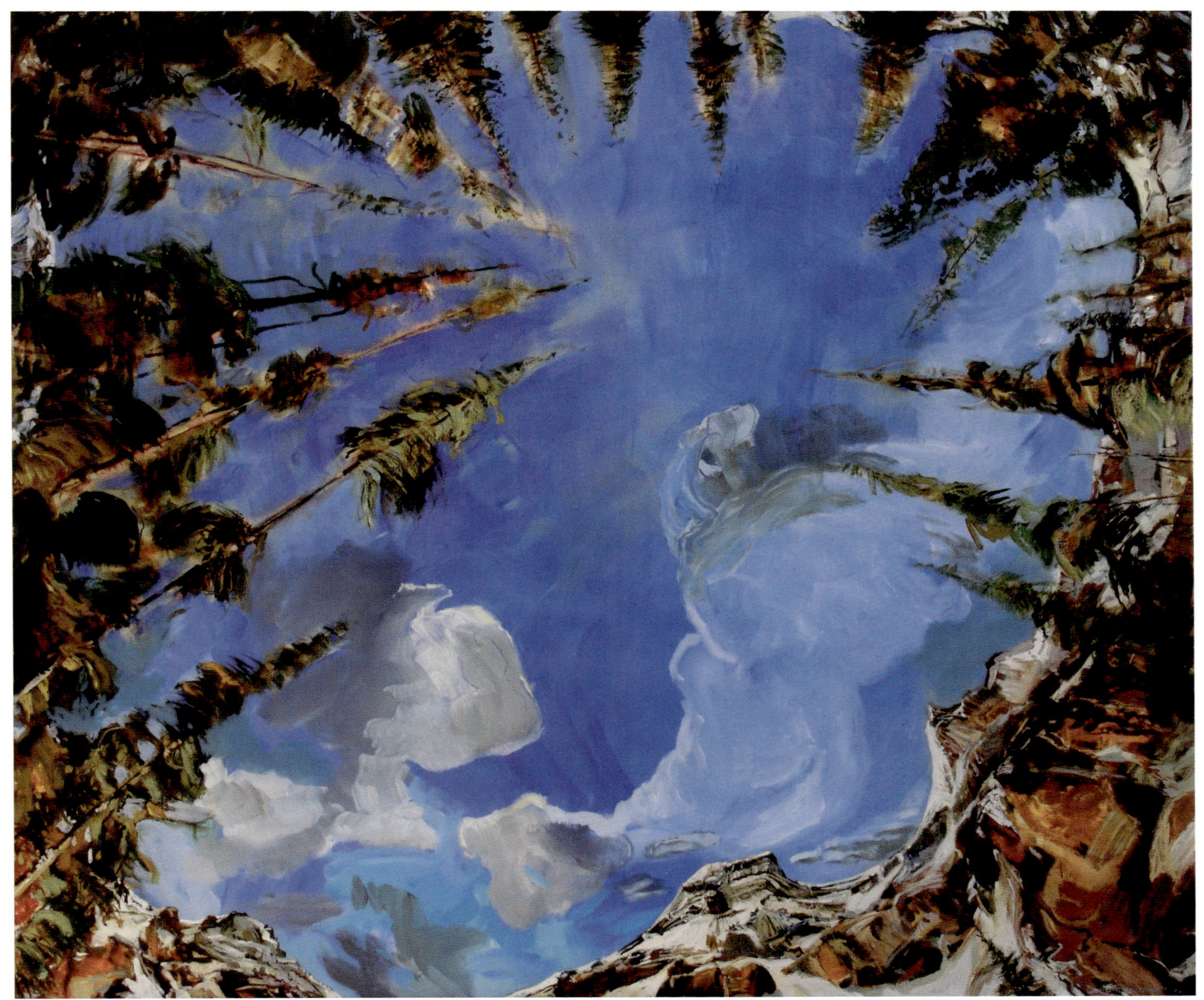

PLATE 25

Mountain Spin, 2006, acrylic on canvas, 52 × 58 in.

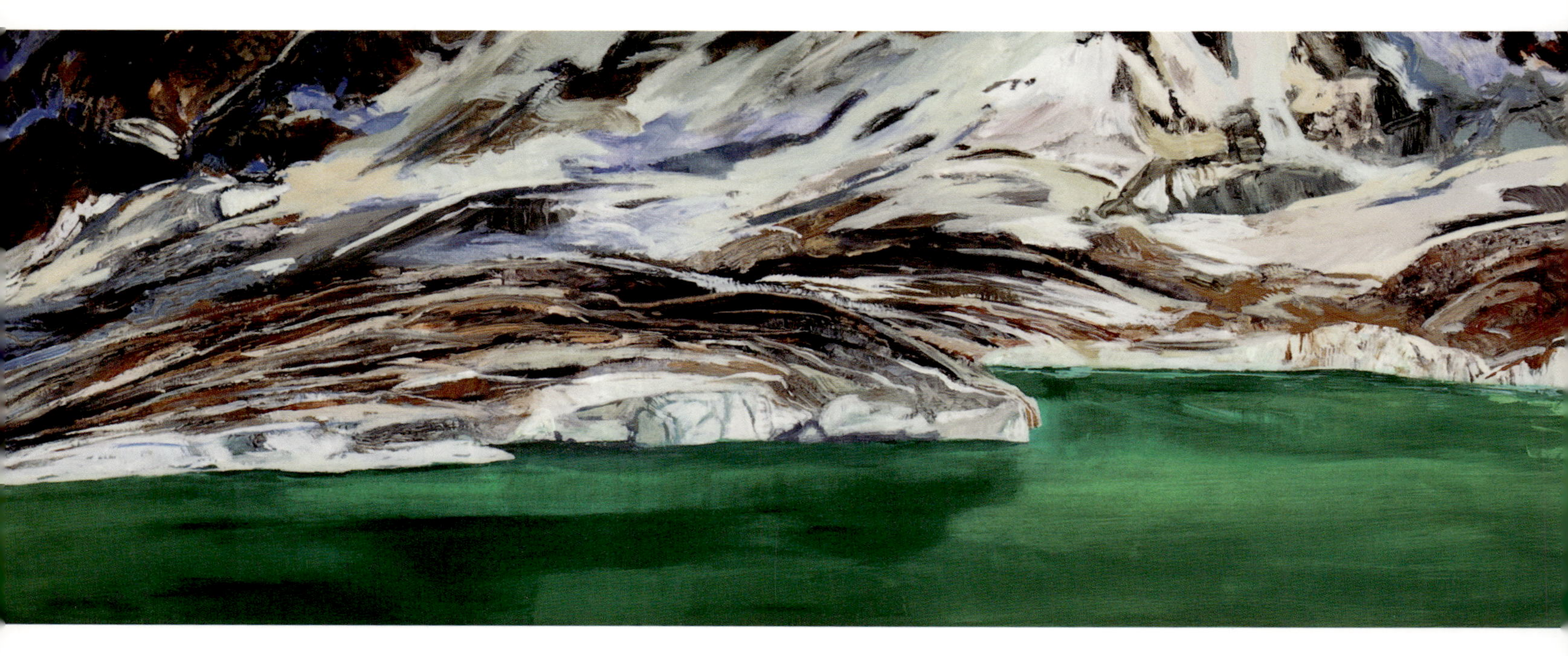

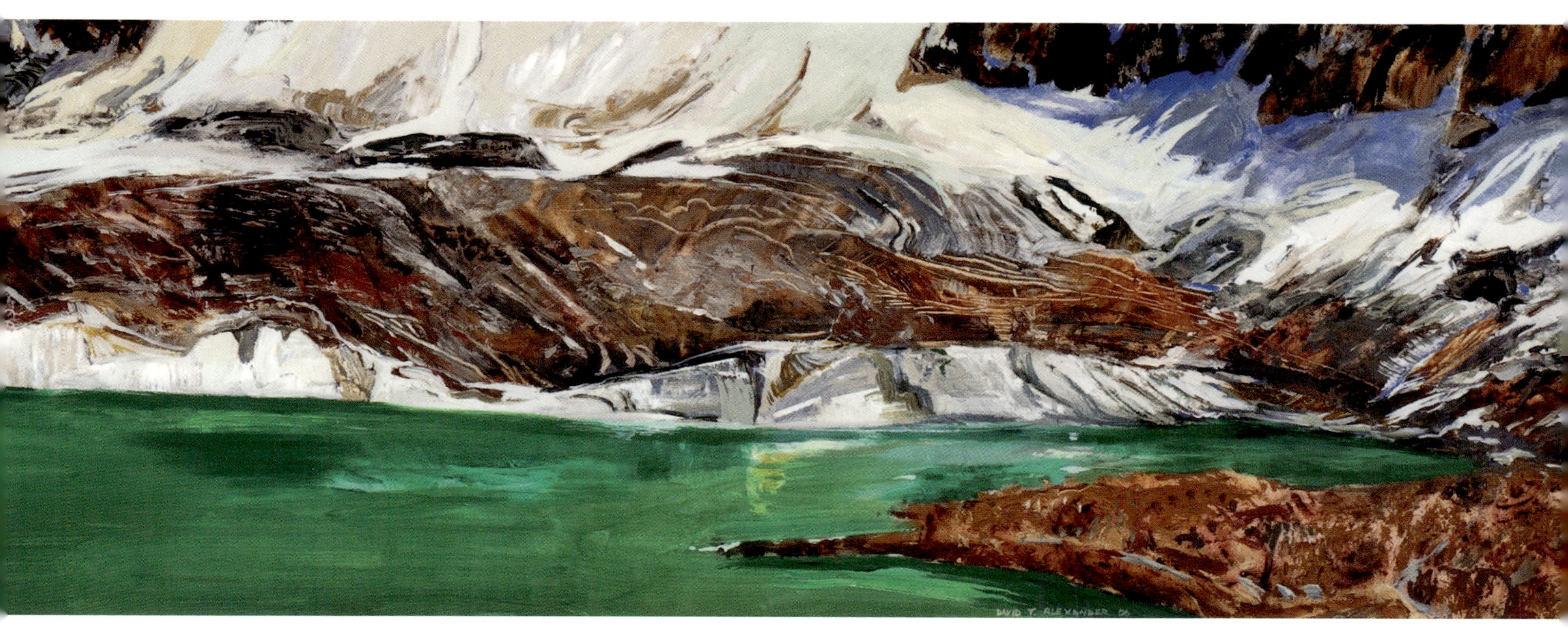

PLATE 26

Edith's Dirty Toes, 2006, acrylic on canvas, 24 × 125 in.

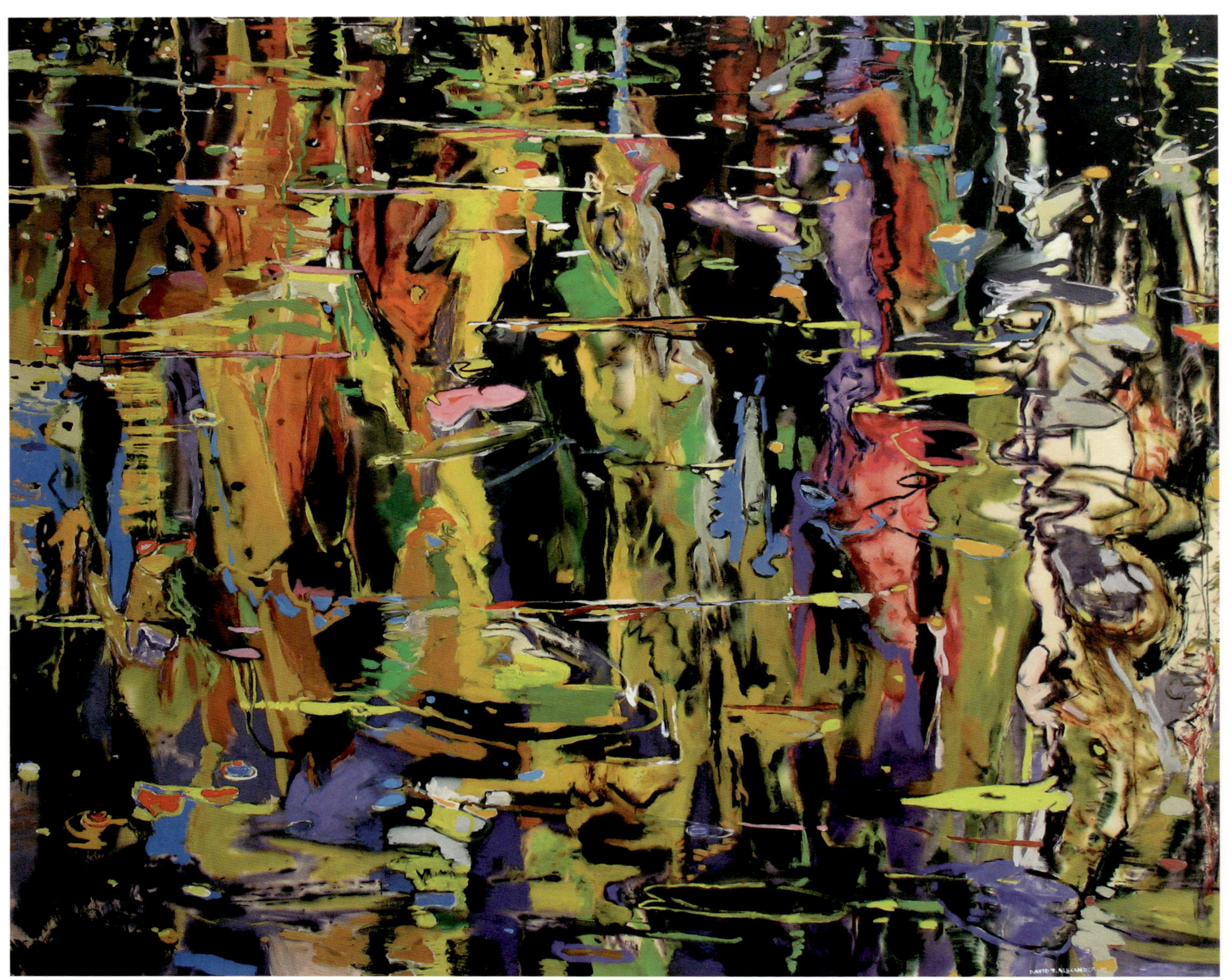

PLATE 27

An Hour Before the Wind Blows the Colour Away, 2007, acrylic on canvas, 78 × 96 in.

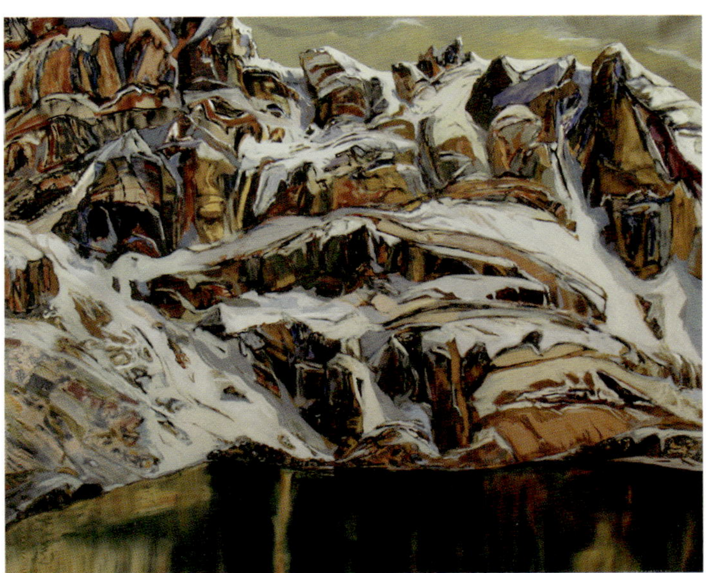

McArthur, Lake O'Hara, 2007, acrylic on canvas, 78 × 96 in.

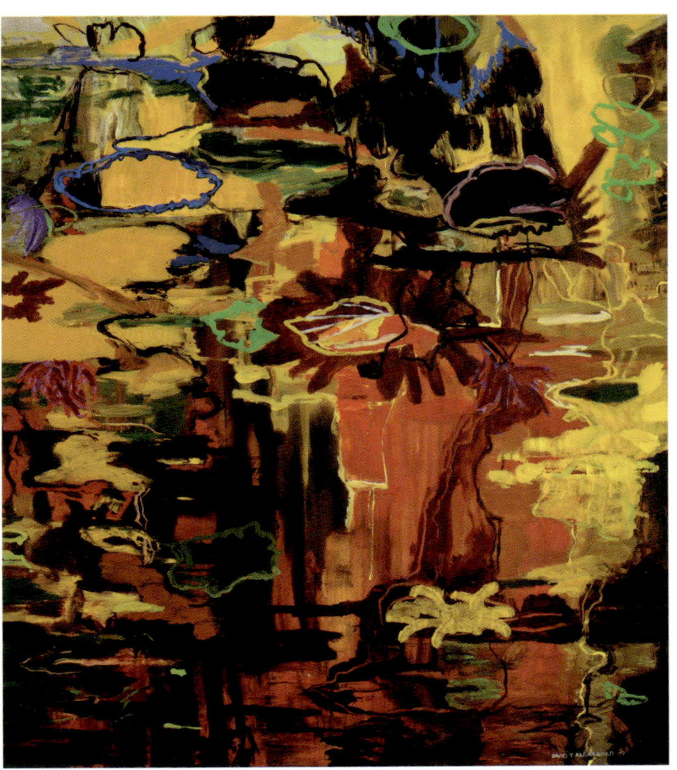

Tropical Punched, 2007, acrylic on canvas, 66 × 57 in.

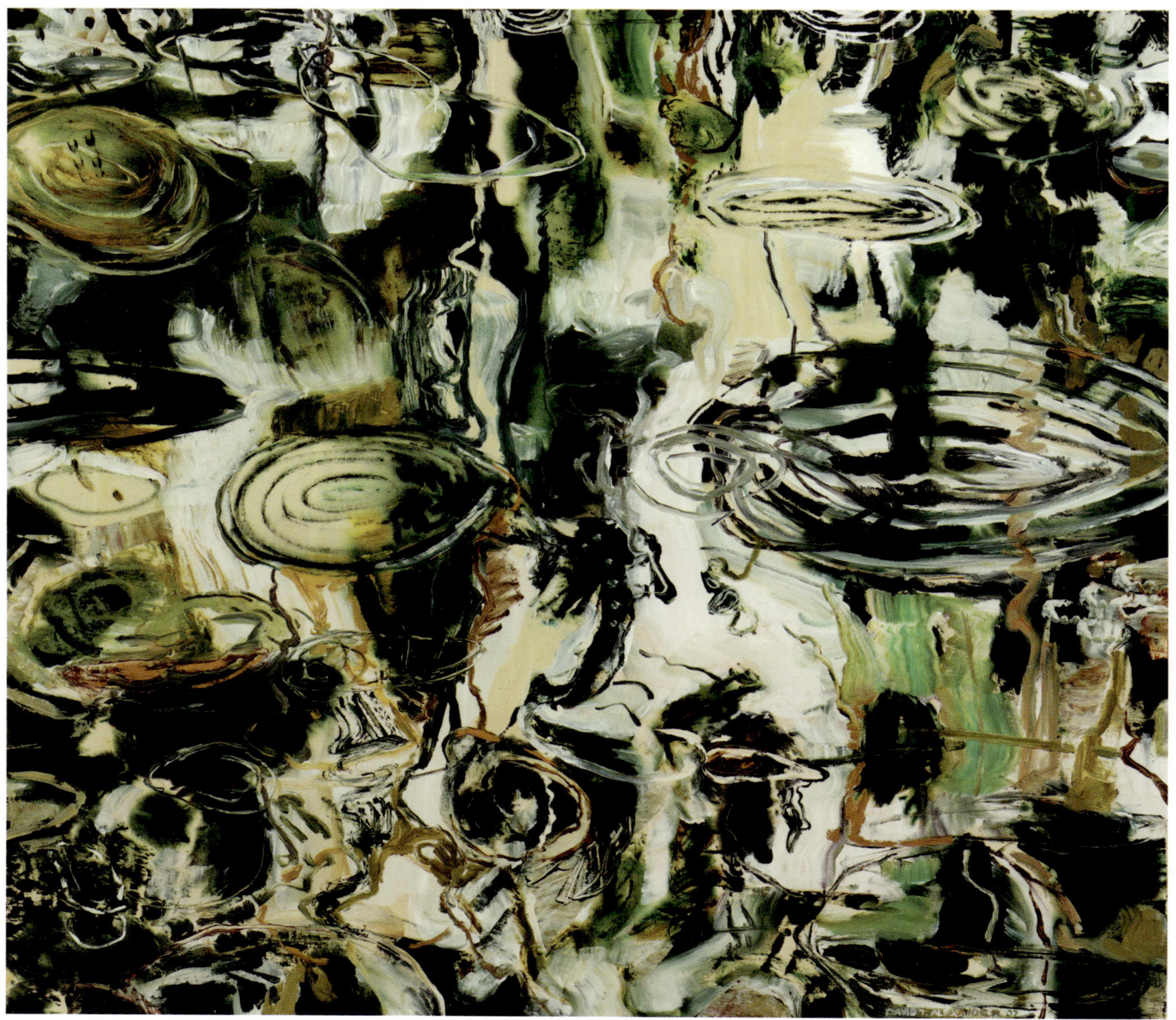

PLATE 30

Japanese Rain, Shinjuku, Gyoen, Tokyo, 2007, acrylic on canvas, 52 × 58 in.

An Interview with the Artist by Robert Enright

In August of 2010 Robert Enright spent an evening and the following day with David Alexander at his home studio in the Okanagan Valley, on the occasion of the artist's solo show at the Vernon Public Art Gallery. In the resulting interview they touch on topics related to the artist's thinking and work over the last few decades.

ROBERT ENRIGHT: You have jokingly referred to landscape as a four-letter word. How did it earn that unhallowed reputation in your mind?

DAVID ALEXANDER: I think because it has plodded along, no matter what else has happened. For the last fifty years or so it has been in and out of favour. I'm not bemoaning that situation, I'm just acknowledging a lot of misunderstanding. There are people in the art world, like John Elderfield, for example, who have always been in love with landscape. Because he was a curator at the Museum of Modern Art in New York for so long, he was able to present landscape in a larger historical context. On the other side, there is a way of thinking that seeks after the new, and from that perspective landscape becomes a four-letter word.

RE: I sense it's even more complicated than that. The discipline of painting itself has been the subject of a considerable amount of criticism, so not only do you paint, but you paint this outmoded form called landscape. It's as if you're obliged to make a double apology.

DA: I don't know that I would use "apology" because it's too weak a word. But if the inclination is there, I think you have to paint it. It came as a revelation to me years ago when I was sharing a studio with the Saskatoon artist Grant McConnell. He was in the front part of the studio and I was in the back, and one day I yelled "I'm bored," and he said "Well, let's paint each other." So we moved our easels about three feet apart and we painted portraits. When we were finished he looked at mine and said, "Ha, me as a landscape." He was right. So I don't think I can do anything that doesn't look like a landscape. Maybe it is just ingrained. And because I see people within the landscape, I don't need to put them in, since they're already present. One problem is that landscape gets dismissed because people have a preconceived notion of what they think they're going to be looking at. Lately I've witnessed some turnarounds, which makes me think a good deal remains to be learned. There are artists coming up who are doing

unexpected things with landscape. Kim Dorland is bending
and twisting it; his nature can be pink and green, and ugly
and thick. And it's also about paint. He loves to wallow in
paint, as do I.

RE: Dorland's most recent work seems to use the Group of
Seven and nature painting in general, and then he messes with
it. He's playing with the origins of the Canadian landscape.
DA: I think that's very brave, but messing with previous artists
can also be your downfall. The problem is it can become a
bit of a trick. But I think Dorland has the knowledge and
the capacity to continue making promising turns. He stays
within the genre and is making a contribution to its
renewed importance.

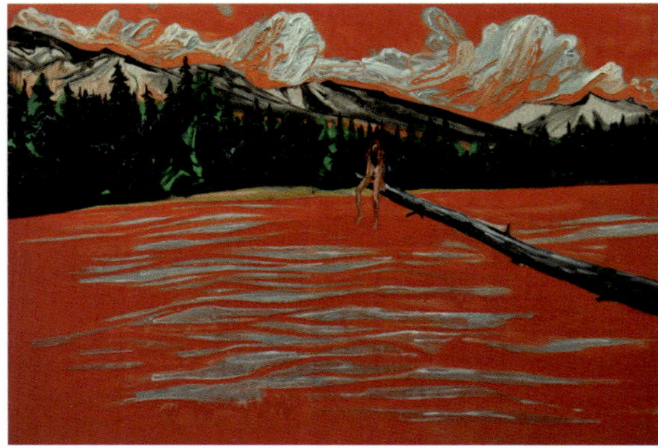

Kim Dorland, *Morning Swim*, 2010, oil on wood panel, 84 × 120 in.
Courtesy of Mike Weiss Gallery, New York, NY.

RE: You've mentioned your admiration for Joan Nelson, a
New York landscape painter who consciously uses other artists
as a point of departure in making her own work. She will
quote from a German artist from the fifteenth century and
then from a modernist. How does she relate to what I want
to call, in a broad way, the tradition of painting?
DA: She adheres to a sense of art history in the way she sur-
veys artists who interest her. She certainly does it more than
I do. I showed with her in 1996 in Sante Fe and that was the
first time I had seen one of her paintings in real life. It was
an absolutely stunning little picture. It blew me away that
she could make a monument out of something that small.
She continues to do it.

RE: How do you yourself determine scale in your painting and
drawing? What's the determining factor in deciding whether
you can work small and aspire towards the monumental,
or work big and let the space carry the viewer's eye through
the piece?
DA: Sheer boredom and absolute drudgery. It was minus
thirty in a Saskatoon winter, and I was all over the place with
these big paintings, trying to decide whether I wanted to continue working from the shoulder. To be truthful, I have never
succumbed to a fear of massive scale and never will. I love tiny
paintings and I love great big ones. For me the problem comes
in changing from one to the other. I'm in the middle of that
process right now. I just can't paint from painting to painting.
I'm sitting here looking at a group of twenty small paintings
and I'm struck with terror. You see, I don't easily get a handle
on what I'm doing. It takes me a long time and it involves a

lot of slogging and then, suddenly, something flips over and I realize I've got something. That's usually a good lead into scale. This body of work could last three or four years and my hope is that the knowledge I gain from those small pictures will come out automatically when I go into large paintings.

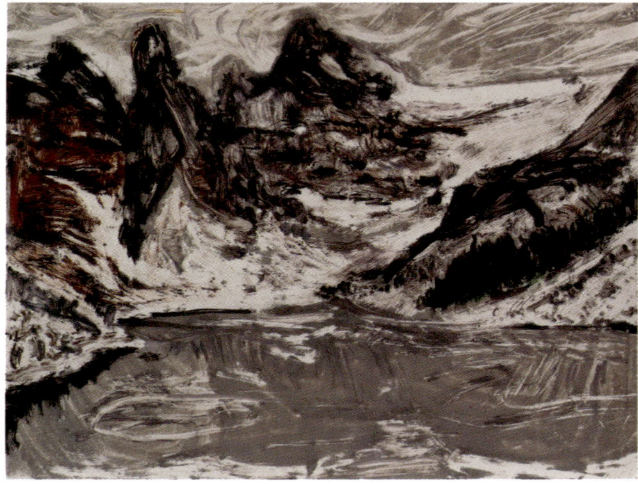

Agnes Lake, Late October [Rockies], 1999, gouache, 8.5 × 11 in.

RE: Using the hand or the shoulder, the amount of pigment on the brush, the pressure of the applied mark – are all those choices in play when you make a mark?

DA: I rely on the tools that I make, like the brushes you've seen that are wrecked and chewed up. I know I can take a tiny brush and make a mark that is a half-inch wide, and I also know I have the brush to make that mark that is eight-inches wide. If you do it enough times, you then have your own

knowledge. I mean, you learn about painting in a number of ways. As an example, I learned how to make watercolour nice and fluid from Cézanne. When he was in Aix-en-Provence, he couldn't do it because the medium dries so quickly. You have to know that. Acrylics also dry quickly, unlike oils, so you have to think differently when you use them. When I work, mark-making plays a very important part in whether the painting becomes small or large. You have knowledge from your own history, and then you look at other artists to see what you can learn from them. It's the baggage of mark-making that you want to travel with.

RE: Is there ever a danger of settling into the habitual because you do know so much about making marks?

DA: I think so. In the 1980s I was making paintings where everything was scratched. I call it my found gel period. It was so enticing and I was so completely involved that I didn't notice that it went on for almost four years. A woman came up to me at an opening in Toronto and said, "We have one of your paintings and I know it's yours because it is completely covered in scratches." You just dig your own hole and this was a deep one. But getting out was easy – it was simply a question of making a conscious decision. So I spent the next year and a half completely getting rid of those scratches. After that, when they came back in, I made sure they had a purpose.

RE: I wonder whether the rhythm of a painting is more a product of observation than invention? I guess I'm really asking whether you feel a sense of responsibility to get right the thing you are looking at?

DA: The rhythm is very important in any landscape. In the last ten years I've been dealing with what I call the *Wet Series*, and they are very different from the rhythm of land because they have to do with visual gravity. To me the difference between the two is clear: one is wet, and the other is dry. I paint that way and I think that way, too. The large paintings start off incredibly wet. The canvas is laid down flat because I'm pouring paint onto it, so if I want to make a drip, I lift it up and gravity takes care of things from that point on. Then I react to that. There are also passages where I use scratch and gel, but in that series I'm always thinking wet. I think my first understanding of that land/water thing was because of my father, who was a tugboat captain. He was like Captain Bligh in the *Caine Mutiny*. He put us to work at a young age.

RE: You're exaggerating. You said the tug was moving so slowly that you drew while you were on board.
DA: You don't know that when you're sixteen. I wanted to be in Vancouver in a club. But the rhythm of land also changes as you live in it and become part of it. I've got to say that where I live now is not my landscape. I can't see this landscape yet, but I'm becoming more accustomed to it.

RE: You have consciously sought out landscapes, from Iceland to Scotland, haven't you?
DA: Yes, I'll go anywhere. An artist-friend of mine called me a landscape slut. The more places in the world I go, the better I understand the geography of the place I'm in. So going away is a learning curve. But I'm also beginning to pine for the prairie after being away from it for six years. I know that I will return to the prairie to work and learn from it. I miss that crystalline light. They talk about the sunny Okanagan but as far as I'm concerned the switch is turned off in November and it gets grey for the winter. Missing the prairies is difficult to explain to people here. The prairie taught me a sense of community and that had a very profound effect on me. People in the prairies think very seriously about what they do. No matter what it is, they don't take it lightly.

RE: I mentioned rhythm because it seems to have had a profound influence on how you make a painting. Emily Carr referred to a "unity of movement," and wrote that for her it was about "the direction of your main movement, the sweep of the whole thing as a unit." Do you set out with some kind of rhythm in mind?
DA: I think that rhythm actually comes physically. It comes from being in the landscape, not sitting back as a voyeur, but actually walking through it, up it, over it, and back over it again. That's when I begin to understand that movement of land. When you look at a mountain from a distance, you don't see the rocks falling down. When you go up there, you realize that everything is moving. So there is a rhythm and it's all about gravity. I marvel at landscape when I'm on my own with a sketchbook up around 10,000 feet in June in the Rockies, and I'm sitting on the north side and I hear this bang. I look over and the whole side of the mountain that has been heated up by the sun is coming down. It makes a mark that follows gravity. Maybe Carr was making reference to the spiritual movement she felt within the forest. I'm always suspicious of artists who see light everywhere, who go into the forest and

don't paint the darkness. On the West Coast, that forest is damn near black. You can hardly see anything, so the good practitioners understood what it was about. It isn't pretty. You've got Devil's Club seven feet high with a spike that'll go through your skin. So there's both real and perceived danger, and psychological danger, and Emily Carr understood that part. So did Munch. They understood their own locales very well.

RE: Carr also talks about the importance of transitions. I'm interested in knowing how they function and what actually calls them into being? I guess a transition is like an interval. If a painting is a perceptual field, then how your eye negotiates the depths, contours, and movements of that space becomes a critical issue. Is it the landscape that gives you that, or is it your sense of invention?

DA: I think it's both, but the landscape is the indicator and my sense of invention follows from that. I have been told that a lot of my landscapes aren't easy. They don't allow the viewer out too far, or for that matter, in too far. What I'm trying to do is locate the perception of the viewer right smack in the middle of this uneasy place, and because it's not downtown Vancouver, you don't have street signs. So what do you pick; where do you go within a painting? I want to keep the viewer in there as long as I can and I've found that going up closer allows you to choose your own route. This is completely different from painting landscape as seen from a car, at the side of the road, ten miles away, or in a bad calendar photograph.

RE: In *A Reflected Northern Saskatchewan Lake* my eye is drawn across the surface, but at the same time I can take visual pleasure in settling into any one of the incidents you have recorded throughout the painting.

DA: Yes, when you go into a landscape there is always a plethora of images in just looking. Sometimes it's too much. As a writer you would understand the idea of editing. I edit carefully enough to know that I'm not just zeroing in on one thing; it's too complex for that. But within that complexity, you get the interval. And the "betweenness," what is in-between those objects, is very important. Like a huge flower sticking right in your face, and behind it are the Rocky Mountains. How do you get back there; how do you link that? The success of the painting is not whether flowers grow there or not, but whether you can work your way through it. You might be confused, but people want to go there, they want to go to the mystery. They don't want to sit on the outside. Sometimes I think landscape painting becomes a way for people not to go in, and there may be some psychological satisfaction in that.

RE: You have a number of paintings in which you place still-life elements in the foreground, behind which a landscape goes on intricately and resolutely. When did you first do that and why did that particular compositional direction interest you?

DA: I think I can sum it up with the word domestication. We always domesticate our land. To start with, it is a very unconscious thing. When you buy a piece of wilderness property the first thing you put down is the comfort zone, which is your house, and then you put on a railing so that you won't fall off the deck into that nasty land. Then you put in a lawn, and then flowers. So you're always domesticating that landscape, or to use an American term, you're conquering it. I think we Canadian-Northern-Europeans are not as interested in conquest.

RE: You actually have a painting called *Place of Domestication*, which raises the question: is painting a way of taming nature or is it a way of paying homage to its inescapable wildness? Not only the title of that painting but the way you often work with landscape involves both those elements. The paintings seem to be about, if not some kind of control over nature, then ways to negotiate its various spaces; while at the same time those spaces ultimately remain inhospitable.
DA: Yes, and I think that is conceptual. The one thing I did learn when I was starting to build a house is that the majority of people will put the house on the most important feature of the land; whereas you should put it on the periphery so you can see the most important feature of the land. I think we do that instinctively. It makes us feel comfortable. I think as northerners we always pine for being in that wilderness and as we know, there is less and less of it. I've been very aware, even when I was young, of being on the edge. Emily Carr and David Milne both seemed to be always on that edge. I'm not saying I have Romantic notions of going to live in the woods by myself, but it's important to have that there. Perhaps when I'm eighty years old I'll still be imaginatively able to go to the top of the mountain.

RE: In a painting like *Rims around the Entrance* or *Iceland's Earth Kitchen*, the flowers are used as a way of edging us towards a space that is clearly dangerous.
DA: That orchid is temptation, but there is also hope. Humans see the beauty in the orchid, but they also see that if they go too near it, they're going to boil in that mud pot. There is that very temporary feeling in a place like Iceland. You're on a landscape, which is like an eggshell, and everything is cracking. The Icelanders flourish in that kind of environment. Two hundred and thirty-eight thousand people living on eggshells. It's like living on the prairies. How come there are so many artists and writers there? How does the prairie breed that? Because it's a dangerous place to stay out in, so people in the winter know what to do. You read, you look, and you wonder. I think artists in Iceland have that same notion and they deal well with danger, even if it is only perceived danger.

RE: Those paintings make me think of the American nineteenth-century painter Martin Johnson Heade, although he would have more likely combined his orchid with a hummingbird or some butterflies. His paintings seem to prettify the landscape, whereas you seem reluctant to move in that direction.
DA: I think prettiness might lead to nostalgia, which is a dangerous place. But, while saying that, I'd love to be able to break that mould. I think we just keep looking outside and thinking, "Now what can I do, where can I go, what can I do with this?" That group of flower paintings was very important because it did lead to something. You look at them and think, "God, that's so beautiful," and then you

look at the landscape and it is so ugly. I find a fascination with that kind of dichotomy. It might have something to do with Zen. The Japanese have a way of putting a twig on a sixteen-foot long wall and making it absolutely noticeable and beautiful.

RE: I get the reason for the title in *Ellesmere Knife Clouds* and I wonder if you're implying anything beyond description?
DA: Absolutely. And that painting wasn't because of Ellesmere. That cloud is the same shape as an ulu, the woman's cutting tool among the Inuit. When I was in Greenland I tried to use one and I immediately cut myself.

RE: So the colour in the painting is blood?
DA: I think that would be up to the viewer. But that's not a cloud, that's a knife and it's dangerous. Anybody who has been up in Ellesmere knows how dangerous the place can be. I am glad I got through it; glad I did it; but I would never go back. I physically couldn't do it now, but it was the most wonderful thing to go through that landscape and see it under twenty-four hour daylight. The absolute nothingness makes it the most elemental place I've ever been besides Iceland. The only thing that belongs there is the muskox. The rest of it is about nothing. It is so incredibly beautiful and can be so vicious at the same time.

RE: So are the drawings and paintings memory prods for you? One wouldn't know in looking at the Ellesmere Island painting that its subject is an almost amputated finger.
DA: In my journals there are pages with daily notations on

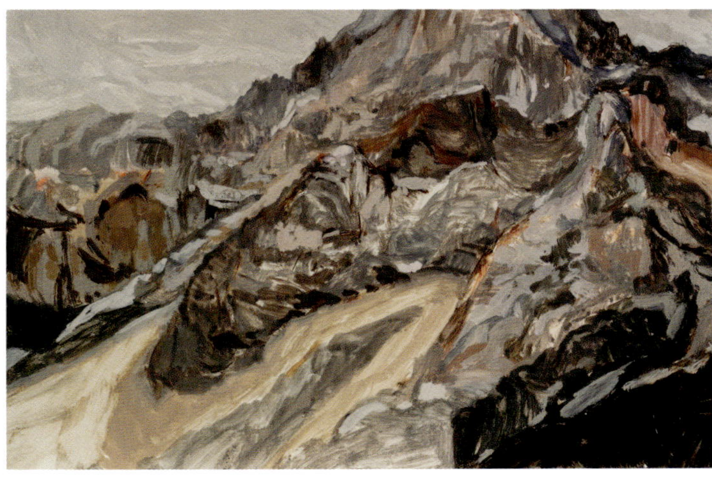

Shale and Screes in Arctic [Ellesmere Island], 2001, gouache and ink, 6.5 × 9.75 in.

them. You can hardly make anything out of them, other than that was how I was thinking at the time. Once in a while I'll go into them. But with the Ellesmere painting I went to the image and I was right back there. I remember when I was looking at those clouds to do the drawing, my feet were shredded and they hurt. So you're dressing your feet twice a day because a grain of sand will cut up your foot and you've got fifteen more days to hike. So the journal is a recall and a lot of paintings recall for me what I was doing and what I was thinking. So the painting, *Not Much Belongs in the Arctic* is not about a flower; it's about the idea of sitting at the side of a lake by myself, not a whisper of wind, not a soul around for 800 miles, and all I can see as I'm wandering through this hostile landscape is an orchid? It's about memory.

RE: So what memory does *The Continuous Prairie Target Practice* conjure up for you?

DA: A storm, one that could be within a person or within the landscape. All I knew about the prairie when I first moved there was that storms come out of nowhere, and there is almost one cloud for every person. Also, I had that yellow canoe, which I put it in a lot of works.

RE: While your work is neither on wood nor routed, it makes me think Peter Doig meets Paterson Ewen. The way the paint is put down becomes almost structural.

DA: I think there's a comfort in knowing that other people think and do things in a similar fashion, but with their own intuitions and vision. In some sense, there is a bit of David Milne going on as well.

RE: So the target practice is nature picking out anyone who might be in that canoe?

DA: Or any other thing. You're out enjoying it and all of a sudden the sky opens, or that tornado comes in. There's always ever-present danger. But you know, we make our own danger. *Real Men's Picnic #1* is a painting that is very similar, only in reverse. It is the danger of man and not of nature.

RE: You seem to see landscape as a container for everything.

DA: It is our big vessel into which we put both good and bad things.

RE: On the other hand, *Backing Idabel Falls* is an absolute confection of a painting. The more I looked at it, the more

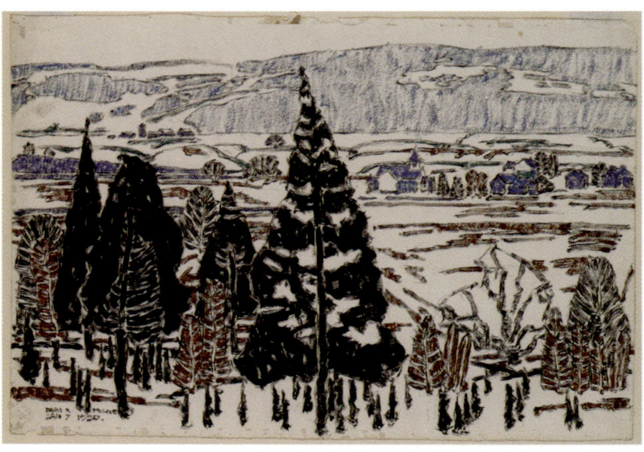

David B. Milne, *Village in the Valley, Black Cedars (From the Painting House II)*, 1920, watercolour over graphite on wove paper, 15.2 × 21.9 in. Photo © NGC.

I was reminded of a coloratura soprano sustaining a melodic line. It perfectly moves across one side to the other.

DA: As you said that I instantly thought of two things: the sheer visualness of Jack Bush's abstraction, and how much I would have loved to put Glenn Gould on a piano, in a boat, on that lake. He would have composed something in eight minutes. It was just that kind of day. It didn't need me, but I had the luxury of being there and making it into something that became important for me.

RE: I think of *Tropical Punched*, which pushes into abstraction by way of surface incident and palette. When I look at your photographic sources I appreciate that some of what you are doing is transcription. You don't need to invent, given the abstract richness of the photographs. I was intrigued to read what the late British painter Ivon Hitchens said when he left his bombed-out studio to go to the countryside around Sussex and began to paint the woodlands: "With permanent roots in this soul it led me to a deeper search for the more abstract elements of the given subjects." When he finds rootedness in the landscape, he moves towards abstraction and not towards representation. You never push things that way.

DA: I understood why he did that and I think it is for the same reason that Monet did what he did. I don't even see the abstraction. I used to say to people that it's not about abstraction; it's about representation. But I have to clarify that and say it is a degree of abstraction from representational things. Hitchens' copse of trees is not trees. It's a place where one's eyes go. I always think of a path; you're in it already and it has to have an interesting way of winding through, and there has to be something at the end as a result of having gone through. I think Hitchens built his own world. He was fortunate. Nature made him move and he paid attention, not to the actual look of it, but to what the things were that made him feel that.

RE: He did say he was not interested in representing the facts until he got what he called "visual music."

DA: In *Tropical Punched* I kept looking at what I thought were lily pads, which turned out to be barbed wire or could be some reference to the crown of thorns. They're dark blotches. They actually do happen in nature. But there are flowers; there's the sense of an abyss, of the change of surface caused by the wind conditions; there's the lily pad effect on water. I think Monet absolutely needed to look at that surface of water, and the water lilies stayed looking like water lilies. I have no reason to keep mine looking like water lilies.

RE: So in *Quixotic Shifts of Lily Livered Yellow*, you're able to shift into an entirely different series of associations and possible references?

DA: Exactly and there is an allowance to do that. Where do you take the tradition of landscape painting past a Monet picture of water lilies if you're dealing with water and water lilies? I spent a great deal of time studying both the paintings and locations of Monet. I can still look at work by people whom I have thought about very closely and get thrilled about it. I wonder how someone like Ernst Ludwig Kirchner ever got away with those harsh angles? They reflected the time he lived in, just as being poor and living in the dark forest of her mind and reality, affected Emily Carr. I keep going back to them, and also coming forward to an artist like Cy Twombly. When I look at his nature, the nature of nature, I know that it came from a long way away in his long past.

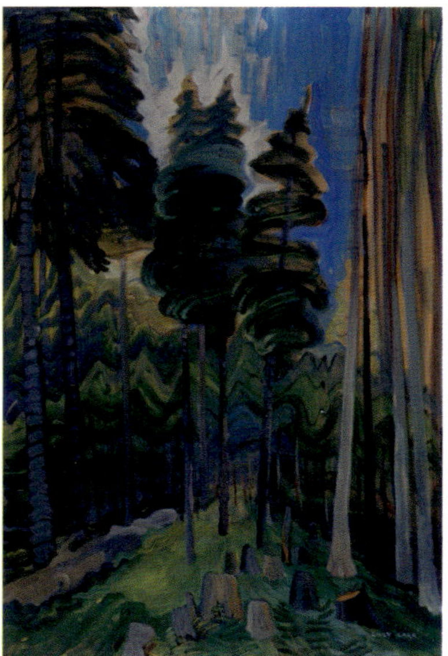

Emily Carr, *Forest Landscape No. 1*, 1939, oil on wove paper, mounted on plywood, 36 × 24 in. Photo © NGC.

RE: I assume it is also critical that you get away from the influence of artists who have affected you? I think Jack Shadbolt called it "exorcising the spell" of Emily Carr, as if some sort of aesthetic possession had gone on. He had to literally cast her out before he could go further.

DA: You do, but if you say that in public they think you don't like the work. I did a painting in the 1980s called *Emily, You're Almost Off My Back*.

RE: The literary critic, Harold Bloom, talks about the anxiety of influence. I have a sense that for you influence hasn't been an anxiety.

DA: I don't see anxiety as being part of it. There are moments of sheer fright when somebody says "that looks exactly like Milne," but I don't terrorize myself by spending too much time being thwarted by a spell. Sometimes it doesn't come so easily, but the quest is to find the "me."

RE: So when you name a painting *Towards a New Landscape*, are you addressing a specific wish for that painting, or do you have a larger aesthetic project in mind?

DA: It's a huge aesthetic thing. I'm always looking. I found out that David Milne early on was greatly influenced by Maurice Prendergast, so I made it a personal quest to look at Prendergast's work and then I wondered where he came from. There are lineages of influence. But no more weight can be put on a young artist than Eric Fischl shows us in his painting, *The Sheer Weight of History*. As an artist you have to make it past that and realize there is more "me" in there than the influences that made me.

RE: You said you learned about the beauty of paint and what it feels like to put paint on from Ivon Hitchens.

DA: Yes, fear nothing. I'd love to have been a fly on his wall just to watch him paint.

RE: In your *Sun Up Northern Glare*, that crazy sun makes me think of painters like Kokoschka and Soutine.

DA: More Soutine. I remember the first touch in that painting, which was the sun. I was up at Emma Lake and I lay awake all night thinking, "What am I going to do?" I got up and I took that red-orange, I painted a dot, and I said, "Okay, now deal with that, that's the prairie sun, that's the sun up." The whole painting surrounds that sun. The prairie was all about that to me; the incessant light, the sun glaring, blaring and wilting things. So that painting came out of a notion of fear.

RE: I want to assign a certain expressionist quality to it, as in the watercolours of Emil Nolde.

DA: Of course. That picture is like a watercolour, there's a lot of drawing in it. I keep the knowledge of Nolde and other expressionist artists like Rainer Fetting and Erich Heckel. I still embrace that Northern European sensibility, but I also embrace that French quality, the luxury and the hedonistic quality of Matisse.

RE: In the late 1980s and mid-1990s you make the horizon line a bit convex. It's like a bowl turned upside down. What accounted for that particular rendering of a landscape that, in the prairies, tends to be flat rather than oval?

DA: I don't see it that way. I see the earth bent on the horizon. You don't have to be very far up to see the curvature. I think for the most part I was being smart and saying, "I wonder how far I can go with this?" It was simply a dare to myself. Then I put it on canvas and nobody said anything about it, but when I tried to push it a full 360 degrees, it didn't work. There's one painting of a canoe that's sitting on top of the world. It looks like a globe but it also looks like just water. It's completely bent; it was down to 250 degrees. Then I had to quit because that became a bit of a trick. But I really like that curvature because it brings everything back to the viewer; the viewer is an absolute part of it. In *Entering the Beginnings of the Dipper's Horizon*, the canoe in the front is not a canoe, that's me. I remember a group of curators and critics were visiting my studio once and having a conversation about that painting. They were talking about the calamity and the apocalypse of it. And I said, "No, that's the beginning." I guess in religious terms it is a genesis. It was completely the opposite from the way I formulated that picture in my mind. And it has become a signature painting.

RE: What do you do about the fact that you know so much about how to make beauty?
DA: I am insatiable about knowing and doing as much as I can. I think that comes from being my age now and wondering how much I can learn. Not knowing what I am going to learn is probably the best part.

RE: You have said that you go into the landscape to understand it and then you say, "perhaps to translate it." Are you nature's translator?
DA: Maybe I'm Shirley MacLaine. Do I know what I'm doing? I don't think so. I really don't. I look at these current small paintings and I think there are some among them that have some good stuff going. That makes it okay; it leads me to where there's more to learn. I like nothing more than the process of learning and painting. Just the hope of making a better picture keeps me going. All I can really try for is to get to the point where I can say to myself without reservation, that's a good painting.

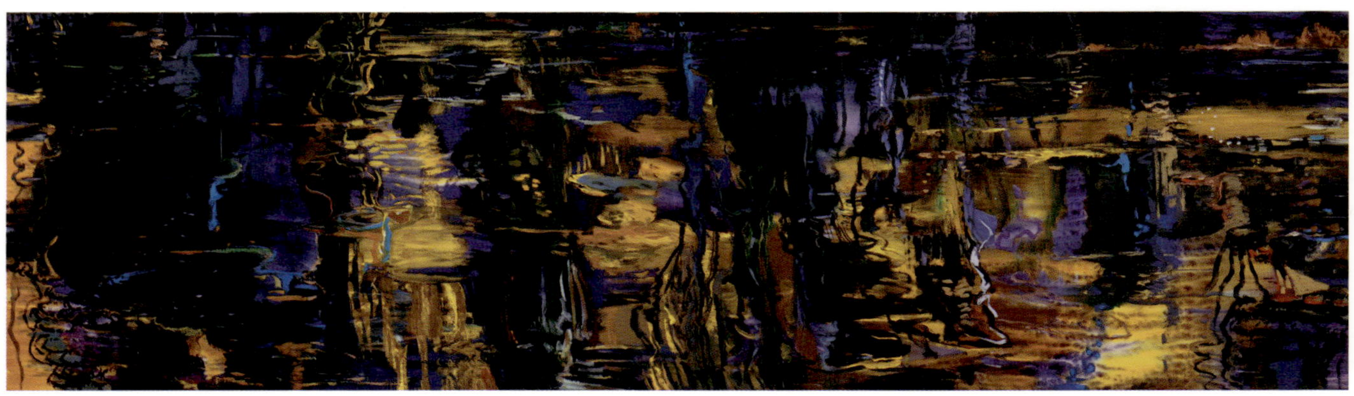

PLATE 31

Quixotic Shifts of Lily-Livered Yellow, 2009, acrylic on canvas, 28 × 96 in.

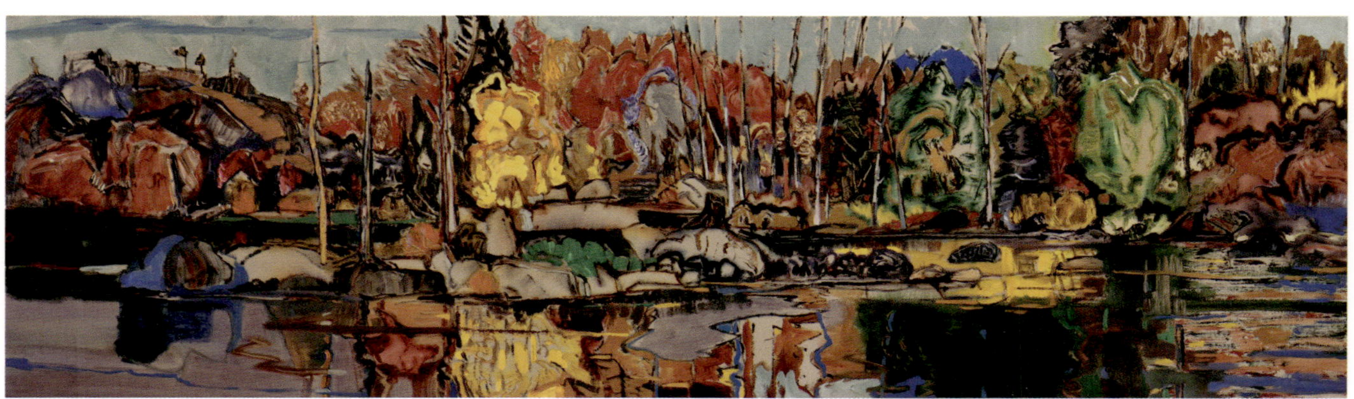

PLATE 32

Backing Idabel Falls, 2009, acrylic on canvas, 28 × 96 in.

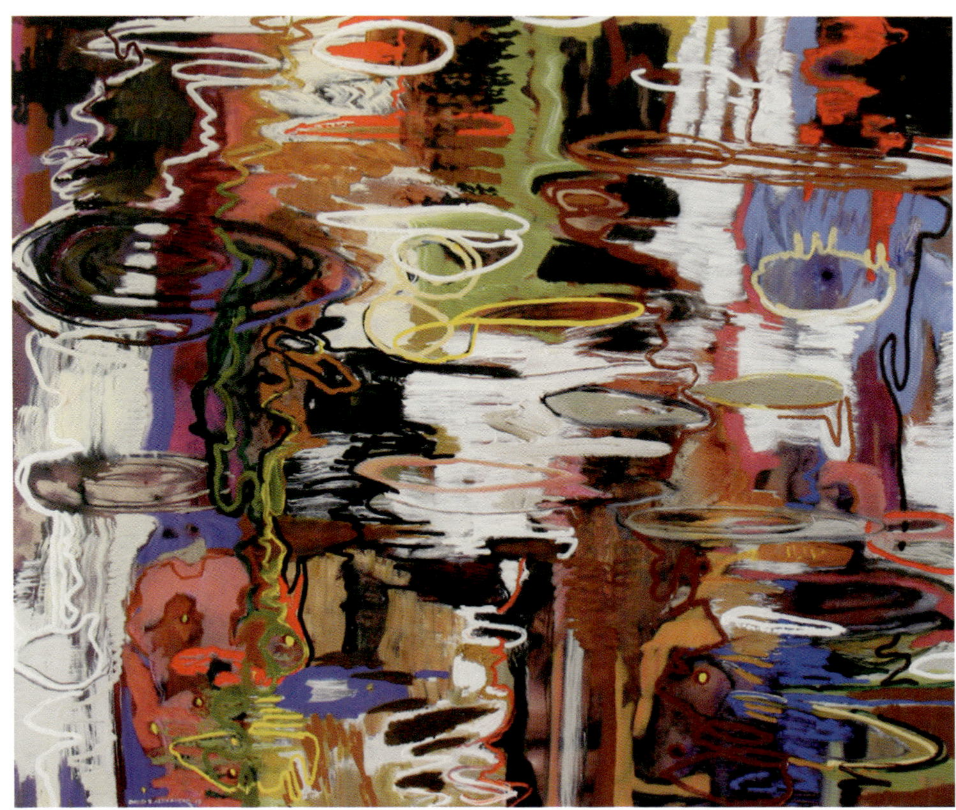

PLATE 33
Drawing in Floats, 2010, acrylic on canvas, 57 × 66 in.

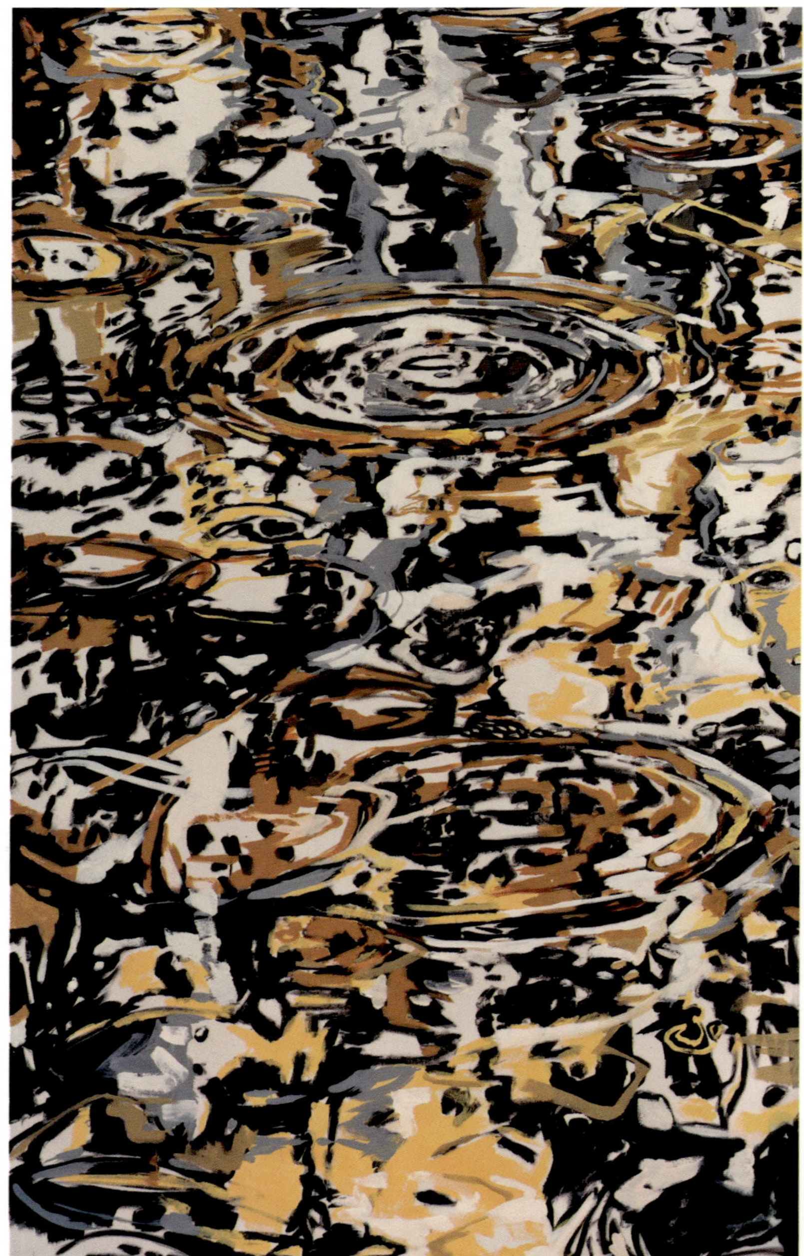

PLATE 34
Salient Rings, Bisque Camouflage, 2009,
acrylic on canvas, 80 × 48 in.

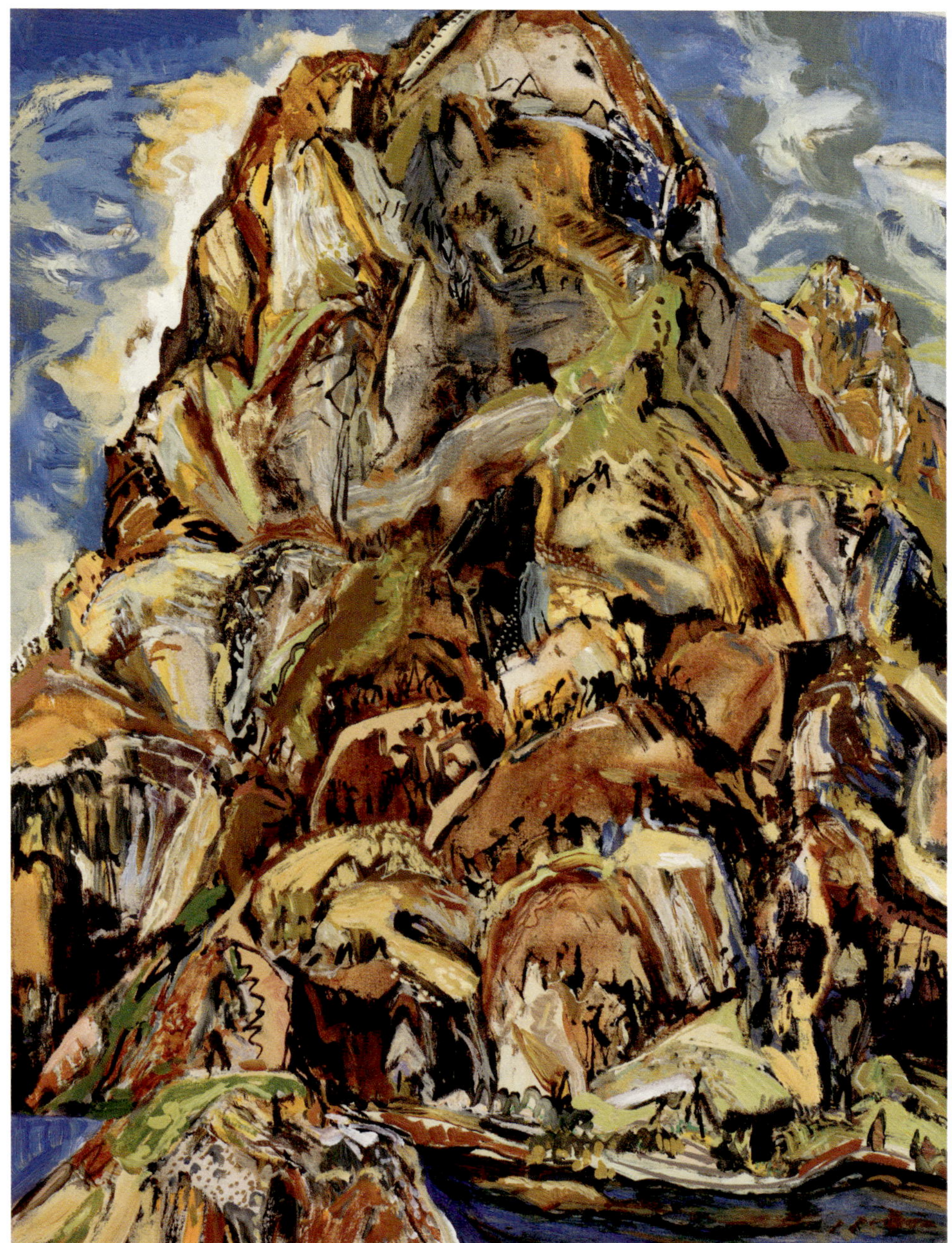

PLATE 35
Fraser's Tower, 2008, acrylic on canvas, 30 × 22 in.

CHRONOLOGY

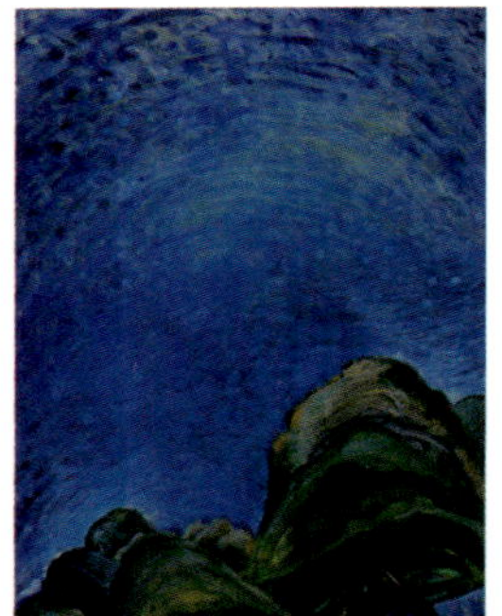

Emily Carr (1871–1945), *Above the Trees*, c. 1939, oil on paper, 35.9 × 23.6 in. Collection of the Vancouver Art Gallery.

CHILDHOOD

Both Alexander's mother and his maternal grandmother were part-time artists. His mother used to visit Emily Carr for tea when she was a child in Victoria. When Alexander was about fifteen years old his brother moved out of the house and the artist was allowed to use the empty bedroom for his own purposes. He kept all his "stuff" in it and used it as a studio. He remembers riding everywhere on his bicycle, drawing in a sketchbook. He was exposed to the work of Emily Carr and also saw landscapes by various BC artists such as Jack Shadbolt and Gordon Smith.

HIGH SCHOOL

Alexander went to high school in the fishing village of Steveston, BC. He had been failing art class and felt his teacher was tough on him. She had spoken to his parents, as she knew he was capable but was not applying himself. His parents took her to his home studio without his knowledge. She then knew he didn't need a pat on the back, but something more aggressive. Alexander appreciated this only in retrospect. He ended up barely passing the subject. He stayed in touch with her after she came to an opening of his at the Heffel Gallery in Vancouver thirty years later and ended up speaking to her on the day she died in the early 2000s.

Towards the end of Alexander's time in high school, a new neighbour moved in who was in his second year at the Vancouver School of Art. Through him, Alexander sat in on Jack Shadbolt's drawing class and met some Vancouver artists that way. He met others, including some of Vancouver's avant garde, at hangouts like The Bunkhouse where beat poets from San Francisco read. He heard musicians like Grace Slick and Jefferson Airplane, Gordon Lightfoot, blues artist John Hammond, and other touring performers from the folk era.

After high school, Alexander continued to live in Steveston. He and some friends opened a nightclub in Richmond called The Catacombs. He painted the stage's backdrop. He was in charge of booking and invited many of the same musicians whom he had heard playing at The Bunkhouse. According to Alexander's recall, the art scene in Vancouver in the mid-1960s was centered right downtown and comprised about forty artists, working in places like the Empire Building. Alexander had a job working at a shoe warehouse on Water Street. Gradually head shops moved into the neighbourhood. Nearby was Bad Boy's Rag Shop, which made outfits for rock stars. There were happenings and counter-culture events, and concerts going on everywhere. He saw Cheech and Chong in their earliest stand-up incarnations. Alexander continued his painting but by the late 1960s had begun to get headaches from using oil paint in a small apartment and switched to acrylic paint which he has used consistently ever since.

He met his future wife Judy at a party. Each of them had arrived there with different dates. They got married when he was twenty three, in 1970. Alexander enrolled at Langara College in Vancouver to study art in for the 1971–2 school year, but later he and Judy wanted a change of scene, so relocated to Nelson, BC in 1975.

UNIVERSITY YEARS

When Alexander moved to Nelson he began his studies at the Kootenay School of Art, which was then affiliated with Notre Dame University in Nelson. He attended for three years, earning his BFA in 1978. There were art students there from the USA, Africa, and also from the Canadian Arctic. Two of his classmates were Canadian artists Chris Cran and Kim Adams. Tony Emery was an instructor in the program (he had been director of the Vancouver Art Gallery from 1967 to 1974) and his office was next to Alexander's studio. Emery saw his work often and was encouraging to him. It was thanks to Emery's suggestion that he find stimulation from elsewhere that Alexander attended the workshop in Emma Lake, Saskatchewan in the summer of 1979. The leaders at Emma Lake that year were art historian and

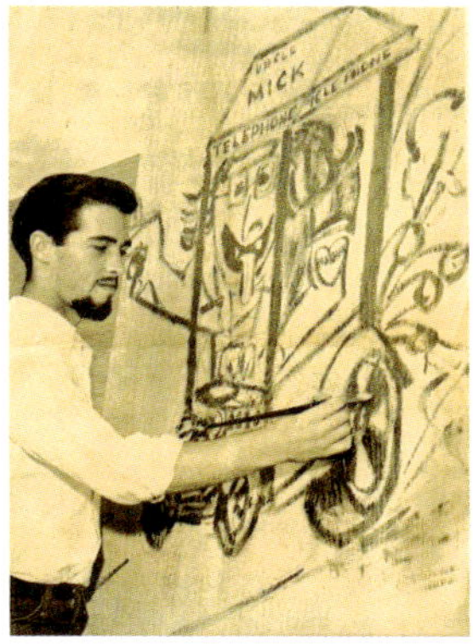

The artist at age seventeen painting on hoarding at a construction site, Steveston, BC.

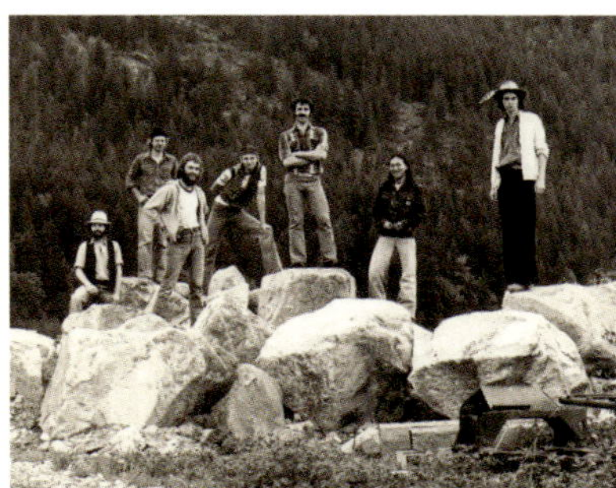

David and artist friends in Nelson, BC, 1970s.

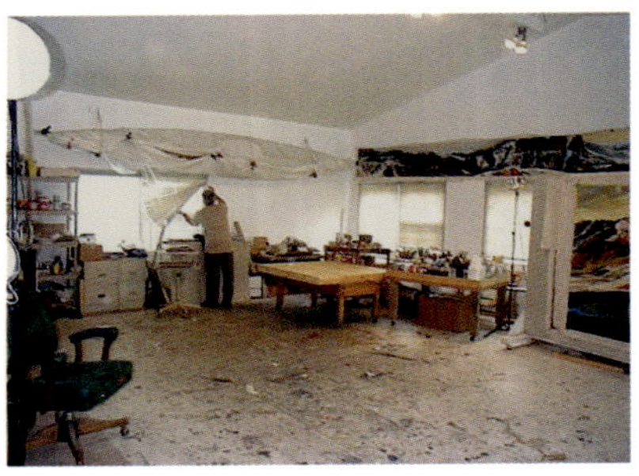

David Alexander in his studio
in Saskatoon, 1990s.

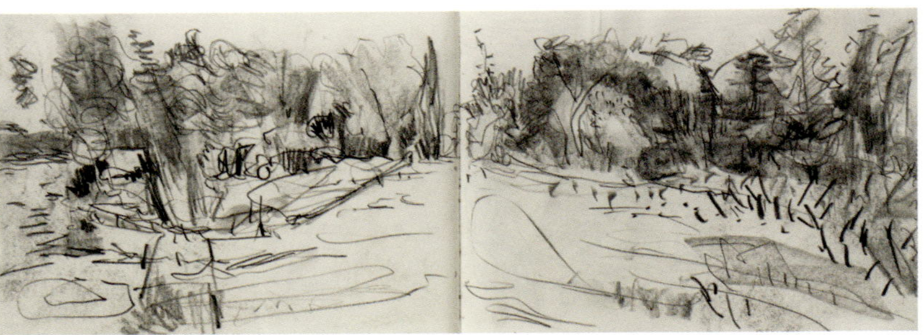

Untitled [Emma Lake], 1989, graphite, 7.5 × 21 in.

curator John Elderfield and American artist Friedl
Dzubas. That summer, Alexander met the artist
who was coordinating the session, Otto Rogers,
who suggested that Alexander come to Saskatoon
and enroll in the MFA program at the University
of Saskatchewan.

SASKATOON, 1980–2003

After his inspirational and supportive experience
at Emma Lake, Alexander and his family moved
to Saskatoon the following summer, in 1980. He
and Judy raised their two children there and Judy
worked as a nurse. Alexander completed his MFA
in 1985. They had intended to stay for two years;
it ended up being twenty-three. Alexander began
to travel as much as possible on a limited budget,
to do research related to his art, to see works of
art, and to meet artists from other parts of Canada
and from abroad. He continued this over the years
and such pursuits are still important to him now.

The other professional artists in Saskatoon
were both supportive and critical of one another's
work. The artists visiting both Emma Lake and
Saskatoon leavened the mix of the place. Alexander
also found himself meeting with and befriending
artists in other fields, such as filmmakers and
writers. He served on the Board of the Mendel
Art Gallery in Saskatoon from 2000 to 2002.
He also continued his involvement with the
Emma Lake workshops, often attending, sometimes working as the session's coordinator for
the University of Saskatchewan. Through these
workshops and attendant studio visits he came
to know critic Karen Wilkin, the late American
artist Stanley Boxer, and the late Canadian artist
Paterson Ewen.

TRAVELS IN THE 1980s

Alexander made it a priority to visit Toronto,
London, New York, Boston, Chicago, and other

centers where he could see art in museums and galleries and meet artists. He learned that if he was able to see the place where an artist had painted, he came to a deeper understanding of that artist's work.

As he began to exhibit his work with Montreal and Toronto dealers he met and befriended the artists who came to his openings, including David Bolduc, Alex Cameron, Joanne Tod, and Paterson Ewen. During his travels he would look up artists whose work he admired and ask to meet with them. He sometimes met artists by sheer accident, as he did with London-based painter Joe Tilson. Noticing spatters of green paint on his glasses frames, he struck up a conversation with this stranger over a cup of tea in Paris' Gare du Nord. He also became acquainted with Elaine de Kooning and met with her in both Paris and New York.

Alexander made several visits to London and to Paris, the south of France, and Giverny (his MFA thesis was about Monet) in the early to mid 1980s. He haunted the museums, wandered in the countryside, and drew in sketchbooks. In Paris he was particularly drawn to the Marmottan Museum and to Musée National Eugène Delacroix, housed in what was the artist's residence and studio. Having met the former Museum of Modern Art Curator John Elderfield at the Emma Lake Workshop of 1979, Alexander continued to stay in touch with him and saw him when he visited New York and Elderfield introduced him to artists there. These included the Scot, John McLean, who lives in London, England. Alexander had met New York art critic Clement Greenberg in Saskatoon on one of his visits there in 1980. Greenberg visited Alexander's studio in 1981, and they continued to see each other socially on the critic's subsequent visits to Saskatoon.

Alexander met the art dealer Theo Waddington in Montreal and Waddington represented Alexander's work for a short time through his London gallery. Alexander would rendezvous with Waddington on his visits to London, and met the British painters John Hoyland and Kenneth Kiff while there.

THE MOUNTAINS OF ALBERTA AND
BRITISH COLUMBIA

During the years that Alexander lived in Saskatoon he traveled to the alpine regions of Alberta and BC almost every year for camping and hiking trips. Twice he travelled by horseback in the Turner Valley region. He would always have a sketchbook along, and these areas were as important to him as the prairie became. Whether in the Monashees, Purcells, Rockies, Selkirks, or other unnamed ranges, he found the experience renewing and exhilarating.

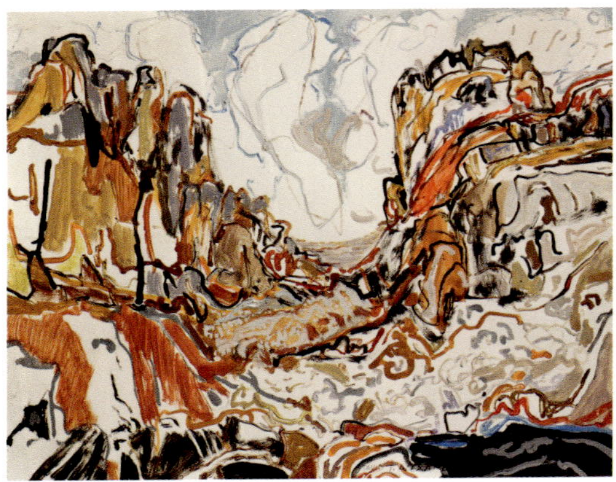

Abbreviated Land [Rockies], 1998, gouache, 8 × 10 in.

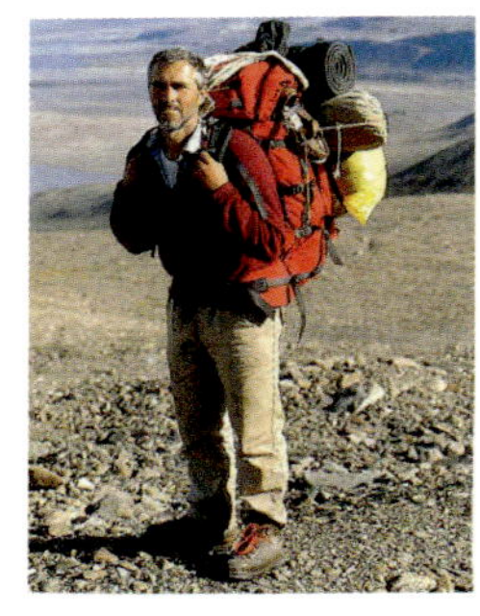

The artist hiking on
Ellesmere Island, 1988.

TRIP TO ELLESMERE ISLAND, 1988

In July of 1988, Alexander flew to Ellsemere Island with a group of about nine people, each from different parts of North America. The whole island is mostly uninhabited except for Grise Fiord (population 141). This was his first visit to the high Arctic. Alexander had heard about the fellow who was guiding the trip and signed up. The group's flight started in Edmonton via Yellowknife, Cambridge Bay, Resolute Bay, then on a small plane to Devon Island, then to Grise Fiord, at the lower part of Ellesmere Island, then to Eureka, then Lake Hazen. The trip there took 32 hours. They hiked from Lake Hazen, the most northerly lake in the world, to a spot on the west coast of the island, Tanquary Fiord. The hike took fifteen days, and they carried everything on their backs, including equipment.

Alexander shared a tent with a doctor from California, with whom he became friends. Alexander took a little sketchbook and drew, as well as taking photographs and writing a journal. The hiking route was through Muskox Way, their route to the West coast. They encountered wolves, Arctic hare, caribou and herds of muskox. They hiked sixteen hours a day over rocky, mountainous terrain, over glacier toes, sometimes with shale slopes, and had to do all the crossing of freezing cold glacial rivers early in the day, as in the afternoon they became torrents. The trip was very demanding but extended Alexander's realization of what he could do. At the time, Alexander's was only the second known group to have hiked this route.

"There is nothing up there that leaves a sense of scale in your mind, no comparison to anything else. Something that looks three hours away can be nine," Alexander recalls. Whenever the group stopped, Alexander would do some drawing, sometimes he could barely stay awake. Once when he was beside a tarn (a pothole lake) that reminded him of Japanese aesthetics, from his time in Steveston, he thought, he visualized a single stem of orchids, and had the idea of putting the two places together. This led to his series of paintings *Improbable Possibilities*, big flowers superimposed over Arctic landscape elements, which were later completed in studio.

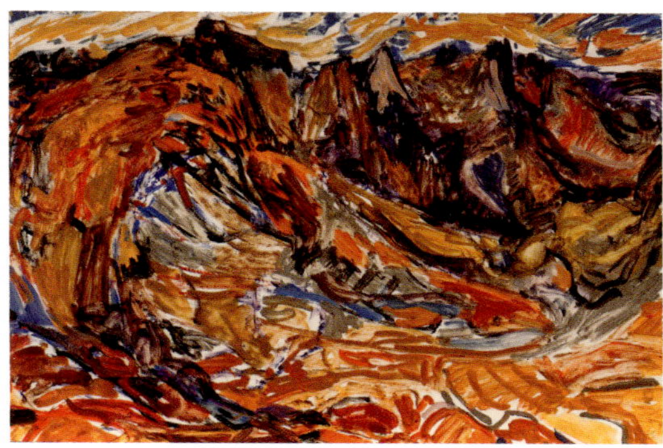

Out from Hazen Lake to Fifteen Days Grunt [Ellesmere Island], 1994, gouache and ink, 6 × 9 in.

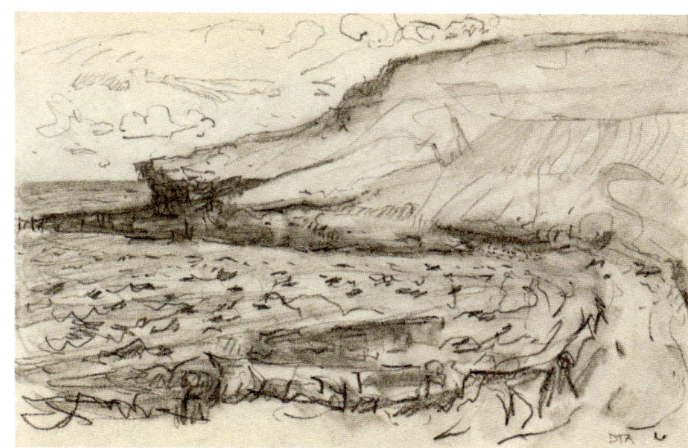

Marwick Head [Orkney Island, Scotland], 1989, graphite, 5.5 × 8.5 in.

ORKNEY ISLAND, 1989

Alexander met Scottish artist James Morrison when he visited Canada in 1988 and 1989. He shared Alexander's studio for a month in Saskatoon and invited Alexander to Montrose on the east coast of Scotland, where he taught art. Morrison contacted an artist colleague on Orkney Island, and Alexander ended up staying on the island for seven weeks. He found the terrain was like Iceland and the Shetlands. He was surprised to discover the historic remnants of a Hudson's Bay Company trading post there. Alexander had a car and traveled about, drawing and meeting other artists, writers, and musicians.

Alexander was subsequently given an exhibition at The Scottish Gallery in Edinburgh in 1991 where paintings from this visit, which he completed later in studio, were displayed. He was the first non-Scottish artist in 155 years to show there. Alexander would later return to northern Scotland.

1990S TRAVELS

Beginning in the 1990s, Alexander's travels were increasingly wilderness trips, fuelling his work by providing new material from remote natural settings. Alexander's thinking about his destinations first began with a notion of nordicity. Some of the impetus from this was from family lore: there were stories and photographs from his father and uncle about their time spent in the Arctic. His uncle had been an engineer on the *Saint Roch*, an RCMP boat that went through the North West Passage. Alexander's father had worked on the Yellowknife Expeditor in the 1940s after the Second World War and sailed on the MacKenzie River and the Beaufort Sea. Alexander's great-

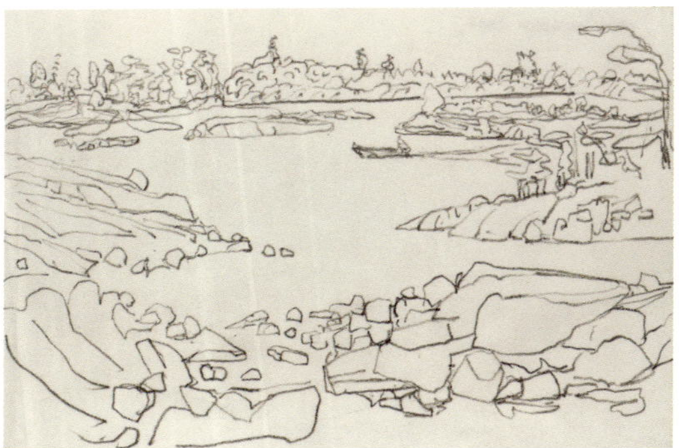

From Hangdog Camp [Ontario], 1991, graphite, 5.5 × 8.5 in.

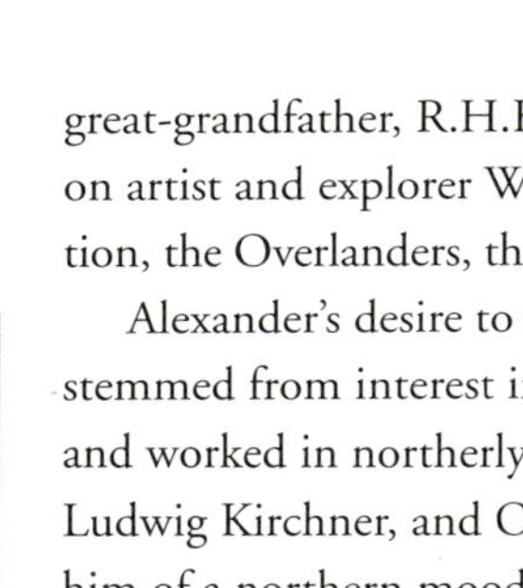

Tom Thomson, *The Hill in Autumn*, 1914, oil on grey wood-pulp board, 8.5 × 10.5 in. Photo © NGC.

great-grandfather, R.H.H. Alexander, had been on artist and explorer William Hind's 1862 expedition, the Overlanders, that explored Canada's West.

Alexander's desire to explore the North also stemmed from interest in artists who had travelled and worked in northerly places: Rockwell Kent, Ludwig Kirchner, and Oscar Kokoskcha spoke to him of a northern mood or sensibility. The Group of Seven were only marginally of interest to him in this regard. He later did develop some affinity for the Group of Seven after some painting trips in Northern Ontario. He especially responded to Tom Thomson's canoe-eye-view oil sketches painted while floating on lakes. Even popular films fed into Alexander's appetite for nordicity; he recalls being greatly impressed and moved by the big expanses shot outdoors in David Lean's 1965 film *Dr. Zhivago*.

GREENLAND AND BAFFIN ISLAND, 1993

In July of 1993, Alexander visited a friend from his graduate school days in Saskatoon, a man originally from India then living in Nuuk, Greenland and working as a painter. From there, he headed up Greenland's west coast, travelling up the fjords by kayak with a group. The trip was led by a female guide based in Ottawa. They paddled double kayaks and Alexander was paired with a very strong partner who was happy to occasionally give Alexander drawing time while he paddled for them both. Alexander was interested to experience firsthand sites important to Norse culture and history. While there are Danes in Greenland there is also a mixture of other cultures. He met people when he was out on the land, and one day in particular, when he had stayed at the tent to draw,

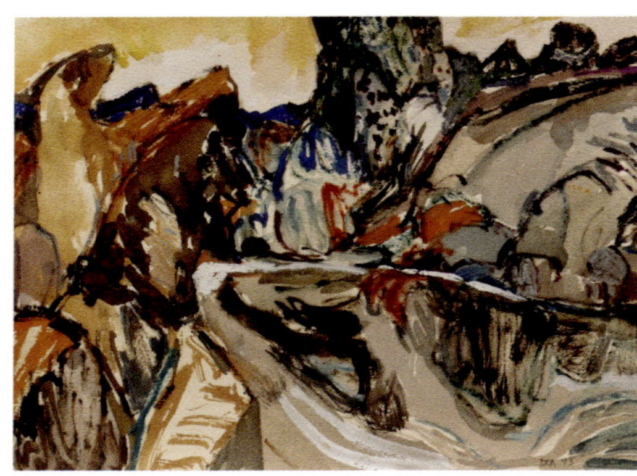

Surrounding [Greenland], 1993, gouache, 8 × 11 in.

a large family came by boat into the bay where he
was camped. They waved him down and he spent
the day with them. Among themselves, they spoke
an Inuit dialect, but one daughter spoke English.
They cooked and ate together, making whale
meat and Arctic char off heated rocks and tea
from leaves and hips. The family lived off the land
in the summer and took Alexander by boat to
where they hunted caribou. This encounter was
an incredibly intense one for Alexander and it
lives on vividly in his memory.

The artist arranged to stop on Baffin Island
on the way home to Saskatoon from Greenland.
He visited Iqaluit and Pangnirtung, where he met
with printmakers and weavers. One day he visited
a lodge overnight and met an elderly Japanese
couple who invited him to their table. The man
was a business executive and liked going to remote
places. The next day, he hired a boat at huge
expense and took Alexander to a park where
he could camp and go on day hikes.

ARIZONA AND NEW MEXICO, 1996
In 1996, Alexander was invited to have work
included in a group exhibition of contemporary
landscape organized by the Gerald Peters Gallery
in Santa Fe, New Mexico. The exhibition later
traveled to other galleries and Alexander traveled
to Santa Fe and into Arizona as well. He visited
the Acoma pueblo in New Mexico, an ancient

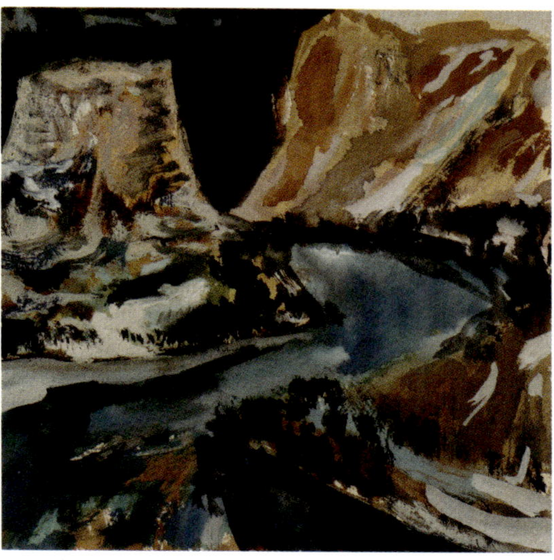

*Out from Pang [Baffin
Island]*, 1993, gouache and
charcoal, 5.75 × 5.75 in.

habitation still populated and the site where
Acoma pottery is produced. He also visited the
Hulse/Warman Gallery just outside of Taos, New
Mexico, and met sculptor Peter Chinni there.

Another highlight was hiking to a rock out-
crop that bubbles out into the Colorado River
near the Glen Canyon dam, about one hundred
miles from the Grand Canyon. From the river,
one can see old Navajo petroglyphs carved into
the dark stain to reveal the paler rock underneath.

NEWFOUNDLAND, 1998–2002
In the summer of 1998 Alexander was invited
as one of a group of artists to participate in the
artist's residency program at Pouch Cove, Newfoundland. This outport is located on the Avalon
Peninsula north of St John's and is run by James

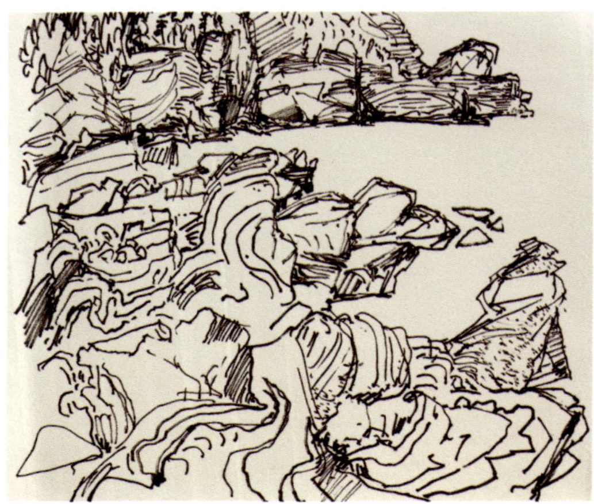

Untitled [Newfoundland movie drawing, Pouch Cove], 2007, ink on paper, 10 × 11.5 in.

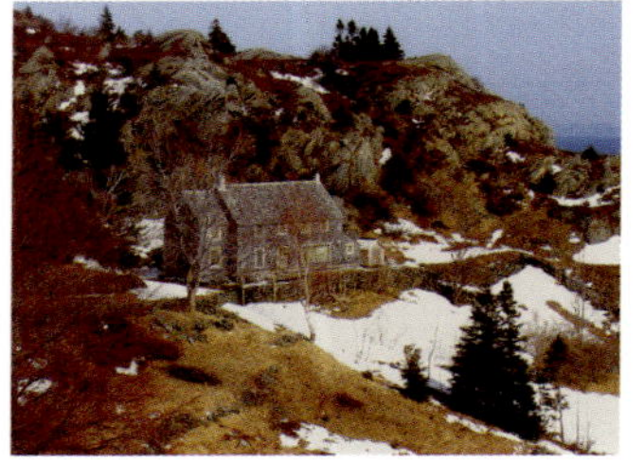

Rockwell Kent's house in Brigus, Newfoundland, photograph by David Alexander, 1999.

the basis of the one depicted by Kent in his painting *The House of Dread*. It was an exciting place and time of discovery for both Alexander and his wife. The contrast between the inhospitable land and dangerous sea and the friendliness of the people was fascinating to him.

ICELAND, 1999 AND 2002

Through Meeka Walsh at *Border Crossings*, Alexander learned that a curator from Iceland, Aðalsteinn Ingólfsson, had seen his work in the magazine and wanted to contact him. Alexander wrote to Ingólfsson and was invited to do an artist's residency at the Hafnarfjörður Arts Centre, not far from Reykjavik. Alexander went for a month in September of 1999, staying at a farmhouse that had been turned into a guest house for visiting artists and used a bicycle to get around and sketch. He also did some painting on paper, in gouache and watercolour. Alexander read Icelandic sagas in English translation, and visited some of the places that were mentioned in them. The landscape was challenging because it was so alien, all boiling and cracking. It felt to the artist like walking on an eggshell and he could often hear rumbling noises coming from underground. A geyser he had sketched near blew up three weeks after he returned to Canada, changing the surrounding landscape completely. He also visited and worked in the area of Eyjafjallajökull, the

Baird as part of his program to promote Canadian artists abroad. Alexander enjoyed meeting local artists and people involved in other cultural enterprises in Newfoundland. He loved the beauty and distinctive rugged quality of the landscape. The following year, he and Judy purchased a small old house on some land in the outport village of Brigus South. They then visited every summer until they moved to the Okanagan in 2003.

Alexander became fascinated with the American artist Rockwell Kent and his time spent in Newfoundland and one day was able to find the house where Kent had lived in Brigus, accessible only by a footpath. This is the building that was volcano that famously erupted in 2010. During the third week of his first visit in 1999, the director of the Hafnarfjörður Arts Centre came to meet with him and curator Aðalsteinn Ingólfsson. She offered Alexander a solo exhibition for 2002 and he began to work towards this when he came back to Canada.

Alexander met several artists while he was there, including the now deceased Gunnar Örn, for whom Alexander later organized a small solo exhibition in 2001 at the Mendel Art Gallery in Saskatoon. When Alexander visited Iceland again in 2002 for his exhibition, he stayed for a month, this time with his wife Judy, and continued working in the landscape. Alexander was deeply impressed by the Icelandic people, their knowledge, education, and awareness, and his visits there completely changed his notions of geographic and cultural periphery.

THE MOVE TO KELOWNA, 2003

When Alexander's wife Judy retired from her nursing career in Saskatoon they began to talk about moving to a warmer climate, perhaps back to their native British Columbia. They found a building site in a small community north of Kelowna, BC, where they built a house and currently live, overlooking Lake Okanagan. Since moving to Kelowna, Alexander has continued travelling to practice his art.

MORRIS GRAVES FOUNDATION, LOLETA, CALIFORNIA, 2006

Alexander became familiar with the work of the American artist Morris Graves beginning in the late 1960s in Vancouver. Graves was a solitary, reclusive artist who lived on the West Coast of the United States. Graves stumbled upon the location of his studio while hiking; it is now the location of the Morris Graves Foundation retreats in Loleta, California. Alexander applied for a residency, was accepted, and worked there for three weeks in September of 2006. Staying in Graves' former studio on the shore of "The Lake," Alexander found the setting sylvan, intimate, and serene. He worked without interruption for eighteen to twenty hours a day, thinking he accomplished about a year's worth of work in his short stay.

ARGENTINA, OCTOBER–NOVEMBER 2008

Alexander was spurred to explore Argentina based on reports of its interesting landforms and similarities to the Okanagan Valley. He was invited to stay with a former art dealer of his, Robert Vanderleelie, in the Mendoza province. Alexander explored the region extensively by car and did drawings on the spot. He responded to the Sierra Pintada mountains, feeling them to be similar to the mountainous areas of the southwestern USA, where he had traveled in the late

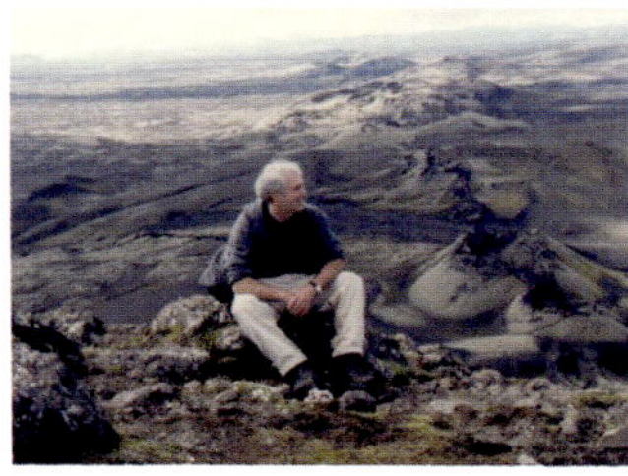

The artist in the Icelandic landscape, 1999.

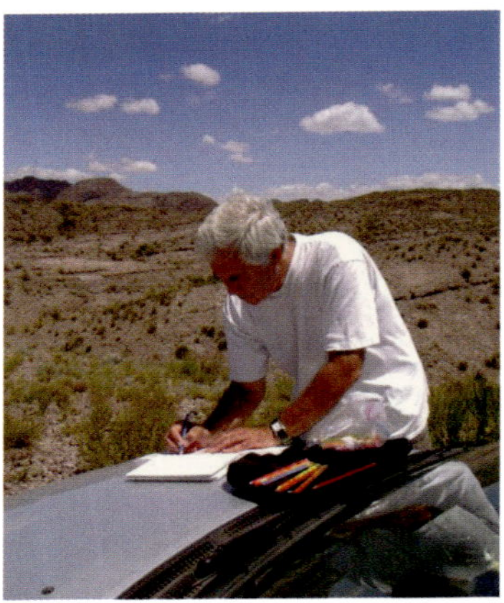

The artist drawing on the hood of his car, Argentina, 2008.

1990s and mid-2000s. Gravel roads that had been built for mining made the back country easily accessible. He was fascinated and excited by ancient ruins left in the landscape, such as the remnants of a thousand-year-old irrigation system used to bring snow melt water down from the Andes. Alexander took numerous photographs of bizarre cloud formations in Argentina.

69 NORD, FALL 2008

Alexander was alerted to an upcoming expedition on a seventy-five foot sailboat that would circumnavigate North America, with the goal of heightening environmental awareness. He contacted the captain, a French man living in Norway, Olivier Pitras, and was invited to take part in the leg of the voyage between Tuktoyaktuk and Point Barrow, Alaska, which allowed him to sail on the Beaufort Sea. All crew members (including many international scientists) took daily shifts at the helm and in the kitchen, and the boat sailed twenty-four hours a day. Alexander still had time to take photographs and do drawings. He felt honoured and grateful to be aboard and learned a great deal about many environmental issues affecting the Arctic region. Some months later, Alexander was able to join the crew again when they landed for a stay in Vancouver and mounted a public educational event at the Vancouver Aquarium.

THE GRAND CANYON, 2010

Alexander had always wanted to explore the Grand Canyon, intrigued by the notion that as one descends into the Canyon the temperature rises. He was accepted for a residency with the National Park and, in May and June of 2010, he stayed in Verkamps, a former trading post at the edge of the canyon. As well as doing drawings during his time there, he also completed a photo essay of visitors and the people who ply their trades with the tourists. The Grand Canyon receives five million visitors per year, and this human aspect was as interesting to Alexander as the geology and landscape features of the canyon.

DAVID ALEXANDER BIBLIOGRAPHY

FILM

David Alexander in series called *Landscape as Muse*. Broadcast on *Bravo, Knowledge*, SCN, CBC CND networks, released March 2008. Produced by Ian Toews.

CATALOGUES AND BOOKS

Arnold, Grant. "Expanding the Tradition," in *David Alexander*. Saskatoon: Mendel Art Gallery, 1985.

Burnett, David and Marilyn Shiff. *Contemporary Canadian Art*. Edmonton: Hurtig Publishers, 1983.

Canadian Artists. Prague: Galerie Pallas, 1983.

David Alexander: Outside In. Edmonton, Alberta: Peter Robertson Gallery, 2008. Essay by Gilbert Bouchard.

Culen, Lubos. "David Alexander: Moving Targets: In Flux," in *David Alexander: Moving Targets: In Flux*. Vernon: Vernon Public Art Gallery, 2010.

Enright, Robert. "The Consolation of Uncertainty: The Vertical Horizontal Paintings of David Alexander," in *David Alexander, One Step Removed*. Edmonton: Vanderleelie Gallery, 1997.

Gussow, Alan and Robert Redford. *Rediscovering the Landscape of the Americas*. Santa Fe: Gerald Peters Corp., 1996.

Harrison, Hazel. *The Encyclopedia of Acrylic Techniques*. London, England: Headline Book Publishers, 1994.

Holubizky, Ihor. "Being Surrounded by Things We Have Not Made," in *David Alexander: Moving Targets: In Flux*. Vernon, BC: Vernon Public Art Gallery, 2010.

Laviolette, Mary Beth. *Contemporary 88 Calgary*. Calgary: Winter Olympic Arts Festival (brochure), 1988.

Murray, Joan. *Canadian Art in the Twentieth Century*. Toronto: Dundurn Press, 1999.

– *The Best of Tom Thomson*. Edmonton: Hurtig Press, 1986.

Newman, Marketa. *Biographical Dictionary of Saskatchewan Artists*. Saskatoon: Fifth House Ltd, 1994, 2–4.

O'Brian, John. *The Flat Side of the Landscape: The Emma Lake Artists' Workshops*. Saskatoon: Mendel Art Gallery, 1989.

O'Flanagan, Robert. *Greenland and Baffin Island Drawings*, Muenster, Saskatchewan: St Peter's College Press, 1993.

Pearson, Gary. "An Hour Before the Wind Blows the Colour Away," in *David T. Alexander*, Vancouver: Bau-Xi Gallery, 2008.

Ring, Dan. "David Alexander: Continental Drift," and published interview in *David Alexander*. Saskatoon: Mendel Art Gallery, 1995.

Udall, Sharyn. *Carr, O'Keeffe, Kahlo: Places of Their Own*. New Haven: Yale University Press, 2001.

Wylie, Liz. *In the Wilds: Canoeing and Canadian Art*. Kleinburg (Ontario): McMichael Canadian Art Collection, 1998.

Zepp, Norman and Michael Parke-Taylor. *The Second Generation: Fourteen Saskatchewan Painters*. Regina: Norman Mackenzie Art Gallery, 1985.

PERIODICAL ARTICLES

Bingham, Russell. "Canadian Contemporary Art: The Current Generation," *Update* (Edmonton Art Gallery newsletter) (July 1983): 2–5.

Bouchard, Gilbert. "Reflections of the Landscape." *Galleries West* 4 no.1 (Spring 2005): 44.

Enright, Robert, "Saskatoon," *Canadian Art* (December 1984): 50–7.

– "The Pride of Influence: a Conversation with David Alexander," *Border Crossings* 16 no. 3 (Summer 1997): 54–65.

Ferguson, Bruce. "Conservatism & Experimentation in Saskatchewan Art," *Arts Manitoba* (Fall 1982): 60–3.

Millard, Peter. "At Cross-roads: Painting in Saskatchewan Art," *Arts Manitoba* (December 1983): 26–32.

Phillips, Carol. "Saskatchewan Open '82: Mendel Art Gallery," *artscanada*, (November 1982): 6.

Sushe, Anne. "David Alexander," *Western Living* (June 1986): 94.

EXHIBITION REVIEWS

Auger, Tim. "The Wonderful and Terrible Power." *The Cairn* (newsletter of the Whyte Museum, Banff, Alberta), January 1997.

Bouchard, Gilbert. "Alexander's paintings keep viewers guessing." *Edmonton Journal*, November 3, 2006.

– "Entry Points." *Edmonton Journal*, May 11, 2001.

– "Pushing the Limit on Landscapes." *Edmonton Journal*, March 14, 2003.

Brennan, Maeve. "Bright & Bold." *Kelowna Daily Courier*, March 14, 1996.

Caldwell, Jennifer. "Super Realistic Landscapes at Keyano." *Fort McMurray Today*, 1999.

Constable, Paul. "David Alexander: Redefining the Canadian Landscape." *Artists in Canada*, November 2, 2003. http://www.artistsincanada.com/php/article.php?id=256 (accessed October 27, 2011)

Dorsey, John. "Shards of Memory Litter 'Landscape.'" *Baltimore Evening Sun*, 1982.

Dorsey, John. "Variety of Styles Converge for 'Landscape' Exhibit." *Baltimore Evening Sun*, September 11, 1987.

Evans, Beth. "Rhythm and Colour." *Vancouver Courier*, April 27, 1983.

Hume, Christopher. "Riotous Landscapes Reveal Painter's Mastery." *Toronto Star*, September 17, 1992.

Hryniuk, Margaret. "Emerging Artists are on Display." *Regina Leader-Post*, March, 1983.

Jacques, Richard. "Vivid Stokes Which can Capture the Wild Landscape." *Edinburgh Scotsman*, November 12, 1991.

Le Gris, Nathalie. "David Alexander, nouvelle saveur de
    l'Ouest." *Le courier médical*, Montreal, July, 1983.

MacPherson, Colleen. "Prairie Legs, Horizontal Footholds
    Didn't Come Easy for Artist David Alexander." *Saskatoon
    StarPhoenix*, February 11, 1995.

McConnell, Clyde. "Review." *Toronto Artpost*, 1985.

Philpott, Kerri. "Keyano Visitor Enjoys Work on the Road."
    Fort McMurray Today, March 24, 1991.

Robertson, Sheila. "Painter Illustrates Routine of Farm."
    Saskatoon StarPhoenix, June, 1982.

– "Poetic Quality Spills into Art." *Saskatoon StarPhoenix*,
    March, 1984.

Taylor, Kate. "Art About." *The Globe and Mail*, September 18,
    1992.

Vaughan-Jackson, Mark. "First Impressions." *St. John's (NL)
    Evening Telegram*, February 13, 1998.

SELECTED SOLO EXHIBITIONS

2011   *My Land Mind: Clues in Place*, Bau-Xi Gallery, Toronto
Foster White Gallery, Seattle, Washington

2010   *Land Anatomy: No Strategy*, Peter Robertson Gallery, Edmonton, Alberta
David Alexander: Moving Targets: In Flux, Vernon Public Art Gallery, Vernon, BC
Bau-Xi Gallery, Toronto

2009   Galerie d'Avignon, Montreal, Quebec
Bau-Xi Gallery, Toronto

2008   *David T. Alexander: An Hour Before the Wind Blows the Colour Away*, Bau-Xi Gallery, Vancouver, BC
Foster White Gallery, Seattle, Washington

2007   *New Pictures*, Bau-Xi Gallery, Toronto
New Paintings, Darrell Bell Gallery, Saskatoon, Saskatchewan

2006   *Far and Wide*, Art Gallery of Alberta, Edmonton Alberta
Recent Paintings, Peter Robertson Gallery, Edmonton, Alberta
Vanderleelie Gallery, Edmonton, Alberta

2005   Galerie d'Avignon, Montreal, Quebec
David Alexander, Recent Work, Virginia Christopher Art Gallery, Calgary, Alberta
New Paintings, Darrell Bell Gallery, Saskatoon, Saskatchewan
Borderless, Michael Gibson Gallery, London, Ontario

2004   *New Paintings*, Bau-Xi Gallery, Toronto
Persistent Ideas from an Imperfect Land, Vanderleelie Gallery, Edmonton, Alberta

2003   Keyano College, Fort McMurray, Alberta

Wanderlust, Kenderdine Gallery, University of Saskatchewan, Saskatoon, Saskatchewan

Recent Paintings, Vanderleelie Gallery, Edmonton, Alberta

Iceland/Canada Paintings Come Home, Wallack Galleries, Ottawa, Ontario

2002   *Paintings by David Alexander*, Hafnarborg Institute of Fine Arts, Reykjavik, Iceland

Ontario Paintings, Michael Gibson Gallery, London, Ontario

2001   *Familiar Grounds*, Vanderleelie Gallery, Edmonton, Alberta

2000   *Improbable Possibilities*, Feheley Fine Arts, Toronto

Vanderleelie Gallery, Edmonton, Alberta

Michael Gibson Gallery, London, Ontario

Improbable Possibilities, Wallack Galleries, Ottawa, Ontario

1999   *Bloom*, Vanderleelie Gallery, Edmonton, Alberta

1998   *David Alexander, Arctic Wanderings*, Feheley Fine Arts, Toronto

Into the Land, Whitman College, Washington State

1997   *David Alexander: One Step Removed*, Whyte Museum, Banff, Alberta; travelled to: Kootenay Art Gallery, Castlegar, BC;

Grand Forks Art Gallery, Grand Forks, BC; Vanderleelie Gallery, Edmonton, Alberta

1996   Virginia Christopher Art Gallery, Calgary, Alberta

1995   *David Alexander: Continental Drift*, Mendel Art Gallery, Saskatoon, Saskatchewan; travelled to: Southern Alberta Art

Gallery, Lethbridge, Alberta; Moose Jaw Museum and Art Gallery, Moose Jaw, Saskatchewan, and the Kelowna Art

Gallery, Kelowna, BC

Vanderleelie Gallery, Edmonton, Alberta

Art Placement Gallery, Saskatoon, Saskatchewan

1994   Feheley Fine Arts, Toronto

New Paintings, Costin & Klintworth Gallery, Toronto

David Alexander, Wallack Galleries, Ottawa, Ontario

1993   *Recent Paintings*, Vanderleelie Gallery, Edmonton, Alberta

New Works, Virginia Christopher Art Gallery, Calgary, Alberta

1992   *New Paintings and Monoprints*, Wallack Galleries, Ottawa, Ontario

Paintings, Costin & Klintworth Gallery, Toronto

Art Placement Gallery, Saskatoon, Saskatchewan

Art First, London, England

1991   *New Works on Paper*, Feheley Fine Arts, Toronto
        Scottish Landscapes, The Scottish Gallery, Edinburgh, Scotland
        Colour Monotypes, Heffel Art Gallery, Vancouver, BC
        A Painter's Decade, Virginia Christopher Galleries, Calgary, Alberta
        Editions, Basel, Switzerland
1990   *David Alexander*, Wallack Galleries, Ottawa, Ontario
        Recent Paintings, Art Placement Gallery, Saskatoon, Saskatchewan
1989   *Recent British Columbia Landscapes*, Heffel Gallery Limited, Vancouver, BC
        North Ellesmere Island, Feheley Fine Arts, Toronto
1988   *From the Landscape*, Alberta College of Art Gallery, Calgary, Alberta
        Waddington & Shiell Gallery, Toronto
        Heffel Fine Arts, Vancouver, BC
1987   Eva Cohen Gallery, Chicago, Illinois
        West Coast Paintings, Heffel Fine Arts, Vancouver, BC
1986   Art Placement Gallery, Saskatoon, Saskatchewan
        David Alexander Monotypes, Waddington & Shiell Gallery, Toronto, Theo Waddington Art Gallery, London, England
1985   *David Alexander*, Elca London Gallery, Montreal, Quebec
        David Alexander: Expanding the Tradition, Mendel Art Gallery, Saskatoon, Saskatchewan; travelled into 1986 to:
        McMaster Museum of Art, McMaster University, Hamilton, Ontario; Edmonton Art Gallery, Edmonton, Alberta;
        Art Gallery of Southern Alberta, Lethbridge, Alberta; Mackenzie Gallery, Regina, Saskatchewan
        Paintings by David Alexander, Waddington & Shiell Gallery, Toronto
        Heffel Fine Arts, Vancouver, BC
1984   Art Placement Gallery, Saskatoon, Saskatchewan
        Elca London Gallery, Montreal, Quebec
1983   *David Alexander*, Dunlop Art Gallery, Regina, Saskatchewan
        Heffel Fine Arts, Vancouver, BC
        Elca London Gallery, Montreal, Quebec

1982   Virginia Christopher Art Gallery, Calgary, Alberta
        Recent Work, David Alexander, Art Placement Gallery, Saskatoon, Saskatchewan
        Elca London Gallery, Montreal, Quebec
        David Alexander, Kenneth G. Heffel Gallery, Vancouver, BC
        Virginia Christopher Galleries, Calgary, Alberta
1981   Art Placement Gallery, Saskatoon, Saskatchewan
1980   *David Alexander: Paintings*, Queen Elizabeth Theatre Gallery, Vancouver, BC
1979   *David Alexander: Paintings and Drawings*, Burnaby Art Gallery, Burnaby, BC
        David Thompson University Centre, Nelson, BC
1978   Notre Dame University, Nelson, BC
        David Alexander: Paintings, DeVooght Art Gallery, Vancouver, BC
1976   *David Alexander: Paintings*, Worthington Art Gallery, Nelson, BC
1966   *New Works*, Peter Ohler Gallery, Richmond, BC

SELECTED GROUP EXHIBITIONS

2010   *Kelowna Collects*, Kelowna Art Gallery, Kelowna, BC
2008   Nickle Arts Museum, University of Calgary, Calgary, Alberta
        Illingworth Kerr Gallery, Alberta College of Art and Design, Calgary, Alberta
        The Big Gift, Glenbow Museum, Calgary, Alberta
        NYC Art Fair, New York City
        New Works, Foster White Gallery, Seattle, Washington
2007   Toronto Art Fair, Toronto
2006   Toronto Art Fair, Toronto
2005   Chicago Art Fair, Chicago, Illinois
        Toronto Art Fair, Toronto
2004   *Recent Works*, Galerie d'Avignon, Montreal, Quebec
        Toronto Art Fair, Toronto
2003   Toronto Art Fair, Toronto
        Waterscapes, Bau-Xi Gallery, Toronto
        London Art Fair, London, England

2002   Toronto Art Fair, Toronto

NYC Art Fair, New York City

1999   *About a Rock*, James Baird Gallery, St John's, Newfoundland, traveled to: Wallack Galleries, Ottawa, Ontario; Vanderleelie Gallery, Edmonton, Alberta

1996   Kenderdine Gallery, Saskatoon, Saskatchewan

Muttart Gallery, Calgary, Alberta

Rediscovering the Landscape of the Americas, Gerald Peters Gallery, Santa Fe, New Mexico; traveled in 1997 and 1998 to: Museum of Art, Tucson, Arizona; Museum of South Texas, Corpus Christi, Texas; Western Washington University, Bellingham, Washington; Memorial Art Gallery, University of Rochester, New York; Gibbes Art Museum, Charleston, South Carolina

1994   *Selections from the Permanent Collection*, Vancouver Art Gallery, Vancouver, BC

Edmonton Art Gallery, Edmonton, Alberta

Musee d'art contemporain de Montreal, Montreal, Quebec

Recent Acquisitions, Art Gallery of Nova Scotia, Halifax, Nova Scotia

University of Lethbridge, Lethbridge, Alberta

Waddington Gorce Gallery, Montreal, Quebec

Burnaby Art Gallery, Burnaby, BC

Mendel Art Gallery, Saskatoon, Saskatchewan

1993   Galerie Pallas, Prague, Czech Republic

1992   *The Hope and Optimism Portfolio*, organized by Magdalen College, Oxford University, Oxford, England, exhibited at the National Museum, Gibraltar; SAGA Grand Palais, Paris, France; Espace Carpeaux, Courbevoie, Paris, France, Cultural Centre, St Tuiden, Belgium; Universiteit Ziekenhuis Gasthuisberg, Leuven, Belgium; Nederland Congresgebouw, JCI European Conference

1991   Mendel Art Gallery, Saskatoon, Saskatchewan

Beaverbrook Art Gallery, Fredericton, New Brunswick

1990   Robert McLaughlin Gallery, Oshawa, Ontario

1988   Alberta College of Art, Calgary, Alberta

1987   *Saskatchewan Art: Tradition and Diversity*, UNB Art Centre, University of New Brunswick, Fredericton, travelled to
        Mount Saint Vincent University Art Gallery, Halifax, Nova Scotia; Owens Art Gallery, Mt Allison University, Sackville,
        New Brunswick, Confederation Art Centre, Charlottetown, PEI
        Waddington & Shiell Gallery, Toronto
        Heffel Fine Art Inc, Vancouver, BC
        Art Placement Gallery, Montreal, Quebec
        G.H. Dalsheimeer Gallery, Baltimore, Maryland
1986   *Out of Saskatchewan*, Expo 86, Vancouver, BC
        Elca London Gallery, Montreal, Quebec
1985   Heffel Fine Art Inc, Vancouver, BC
        Waddington & Shiell Gallery, Toronto
        Canadian Contemporary Art, Edmonton Art Gallery, Edmonton, Alberta
        Fourteen Saskatchewan Painters, MacKenzie Gallery, Regina, Saskatchewan
        Chicago Art Fair, Chicago, Illinois
1984   Elca London Gallery, Montreal, Quebec
        Saskatchewan Open, Mendel Art Gallery, Saskatoon, Saskatchewan
1983   Heffel Fine Arts, Vancouver, BC
        Dunlop Art Gallery, Regina, Saskatchewan
1982   Art Placement Gallery, Saskatoon, Saskatchewan
        Saskatchewan Landscape Painters, Virginia Christopher Art Galleries, Calgary, Alberta
1981   *After Emma*, Edmonton Art Gallery, Edmonton, Alberta, traveled to Snelgrove Gallery, University of Saskatchewan,
        Saskatoon, Saskatchewan
1980   *Drawings by 2*, Mount Royal College, Calgary, Alberta (with Barbara Ballachey)
        Interpretations of the Landscape, Art Placement Gallery, Saskatoon, Saskatchewan
1979   Burnaby Art Gallery, Burnaby, BC
1978   *Graduating Exhibition*, Notre Dame University, Nelson, BC
1977   Topham Brown Gallery, Vernon, BC
1976   Worthington Art Gallery, Nelson, BC
1975   Clockworks Gallery, Nelson, BC

PUBLIC COLLECTIONS

Art Gallery of Alberta, Edmonton, Alberta

Art Gallery of Nova Scotia, Halifax, Nova Scotia

Beaverbrook Art Gallery, Fredericton, New Brunswick

Burnaby Art Gallery, Burnaby, BC

Canada Council Art Bank, Ottawa, Ontario

Canadian Embassy, Beijing, China

Canadian Embassy, Warsaw, Poland

Concordia University, Montreal, Quebec

Department of Foreign Affairs (Canadian Government), Berlin, Germany

Department of Foreign Affairs (Canadian Government), Manila, Philippines and Melbourne, Australia

Dunlop Gallery, Regina, Saskatchewan

Georgian College, Barrie, Ontario

Glenbow Museum, Calgary, Alberta

Grant MacEwan Community College, Edmonton, Alberta

Hafnarborg, Hafnarfjörður, Iceland

Justina M Barnicke Gallery, Hart House, University of Toronto, Toronto

Kelowna Art Gallery, Kelowna, BC

Keyano College, Fort McMurray, Alberta

Mackenzie Art Gallery, Regina, Saskatchewan

MacLaren Art Centre, Barrie, Ontario

McMaster University, Hamilton, Ontario

Mendel Art Gallery, Saskatoon, Saskatchewan

Morris Graves Foundation, Loleta, California

Museum London, London, Ontario

Notre Dame University, Nelson, BC

Robert McLaughlin Gallery, Oshawa, Ontario

Saskatchewan Arts Board Collection, Regina, Saskatchewan

University of British Columbia, Belkin Art Gallery, Vancouver, BC

University of Lethbridge, Lethbridge, Alberta

University of Saskatchewan, Saskatoon, Saskatchewan

Vancouver Art Gallery, Vancouver, BC

Tom Thomson Memorial Art Gallery, Owen Sound, Ontario

CORPORATE COLLECTIONS

Air Canada, Montreal

Armak Chemicals, Toronto

Atelier Baraness & Cawker, Nice, France

BC Gas, Vancouver

BC Lotteries Foundation

Bank of Montreal, Winnipeg, Manitoba

Burroughs Memorex, Inc., Toronto

Canadian General Electric, Toronto

Canadian Imperial Bank of Commerce, Montreal

Capital Guardian (Canada) Inc., Toronto

Dupont Canada, Toronto

Emaar Properties, Dubai, UAE

Esso Resources, Calgary, Alberta

First City Trust, Vancouver

Granite Club, Toronto

Hewlett Packard, Toronto

Hiram Walker, Toronto

Hudson's Bay Oil, Denver, Colorado

Hughes Petroleum, Edmonton, Alberta

Husky Oil, Calgary, Alberta

Imperial Oil, Calgary, Alberta

Korean Energy, Seoul, Korea

Leopold Properties, Montreal

McCarthy Tetrault, Toronto and Vancouver

McLean Hunter Publishers, Toronto

McMillan Binch, Toronto

Nova Corporation, Calgary, Alberta

Osler, Hoskin & Harcourt, Toronto

Pan-Oil, Calgary, Alberta

Petro-Can, Calgary, Alberta

Power Corp., Montreal

Pratt and Whitney, Montreal

Rothchilds Inc.

Royal Bank of Canada

Royal Trust, Montreal

Saskatchewan Potash Corporation, Saskatoon, Saskatchewan

Saskatchewan Telecommunications, Regina, Saskatchewan

Stantec Inc., Edmonton, Alberta

Shell Resources, Calgary, Alberta

Sterling Crane, Edmonton, Alberta

Stikeman Elliott, New York

Suncor Inc., Toronto

Sunlife Assurance, Toronto

Syncrude Canada, Edmonton, Alberta

TD Canada Trust, Toronto

TD Evergreen, Edmonton, Alberta

Teleglobe Canada, Montreal

Trimark Investments, Toronto

Via Rail, Montreal

Waterclub, Toronto

Westbourne Industries, Montreal

Wood Gundy, Edmonton, Alberta

CURATORIAL PROJECTS

Curator, *Artist for Artist, a solo exhibition of work by Gunnar Örn*, Mendel Art Gallery, Saskatoon, Saskatchewan, 2001.

Curator, *About the Rock*, James Baird Gallery, St John's, Newfoundland, traveled to: Wallack Galleries, Ottawa, Ontario; Vanderleelie Gallery, Edmonton, Alberta, 1999

Co-curator, with Kent Archer, *Contemporary Canadian Landscape* exhibition, Kenderdine Gallery, Saskatoon, Saskatchewan, 1997

Co-curator (with John O'Brian, professor of art history at the University of British Columbia, Vancouver), *Gasoline, Oil, and Paper: The 1930s Oil-on-Paper Paintings of Emily Carr*, Saskatoon: Mendel Art Gallery, 1995; travelled to Edmonton Art Gallery.

Curator of *Emma Lake Now*, Frances Morrison Library Gallery, Saskatoon, Saskatchewan, 1982

Gilbert Bouchard was a well-loved cultural commentator and freelance writer who lived and worked in Edmonton. He was a regular contributor to the *Edmonton Journal* and to CBC radio, and was a great community activist and organizer. He tragically died at the age of forty-seven in 2009.

Sharon Butala is the author of nine works of fiction and seven of non-fiction, the best known of which is *The Perfection of the Morning: An Apprenticeship in Nature*. Her work has won many awards. Saskatchewan born, bred, and educated, she currently lives in Calgary, Alberta.

Robert Enright is a Winnipeg-based critic who holds the University Research Chair in Art Theory and Criticism in the School of Fine Art and Music at the University of Guelph. He is also Senior Contributing Editor at *Border Crossings* magazine, in which he has published over 200 interviews with contemporary artists from Canada, the US, and Europe. In 2005 he was made a Member of the Order of Canada.

Ihor Holubizky is an art and cultural historian and essayist. He has worked in Canada and the Americas, Australia, and Europe, and currently is the senior curator for the McMaster Museum of Art at McMaster University in Hamilton, Ontario.

Aðalsteinn Ingólfsson is an art historian, curator, and author of some thirty books on Icelandic and international art and culture. He has also worked as a senior curator at the National Gallery of Iceland, and as director of the Icelandic Museum of Design and Applied Art.

Liz Wylie is curator of the Kelowna Art Gallery in Kelowna, BC. Prior to moving to the Okanagan, she was curator at the University of Toronto Art Centre for eleven years. She has published widely, mostly on historical and contemporary Canadian art.